Profile of Three Theories

Erikson
Maslow
Piaget

Compilation by

Carol Tribe

Child and Family Studies Department
Weber State College
Ogden, Utah

Nyack College - Bailey Library
One South Blvd.
Nyack, NY 10960

KENDALL/HUNT PUBLISHING COMPANY
4050 Westmark Drive   Dubuque, Iowa 52002

CREDITS

Specified excerpts adapted, abridged, and rearranged from pp. 37–38
and 42–47 in *Motivation and Personality*, Second Edition by
Abraham H. Maslow. Copyright © 1970 by Abraham H. Maslow.
Reprinted by permission of Harper and Row, Publishers, Inc.

From *Toward a Psychology of Being* by Abraham H. Maslow.
Copyright © 1968 by Van Nostrand Reinhold. Reprinted by
permission of Van Nostrand Reinhold Company.

From *The Farther Reaches of Human Nature* by Abraham Maslow.
Copyright © 1971 by Bertha Maslow. An Esalen Book. Reprinted by
permission of Viking Penguin, Inc.

Illustrations by Karen Wimmer, Department of Instructional
Development, Weber State College.

CHILD DEVELOPMENT: Compilation of Developmental Theorists
and Child Rearing Practices of Various Cultures
Copyright © 1973 by Carol Tribe

Contents

Introduction

The presentation of theoretical material in textbooks for child development students was traditionally too brief. The constructs of the theorists themselves were too long and elaborate for the beginning student. This compilation consists of organizing a succinct summary—without interpretation or analysis—of the theories of Erikson, Maslow, and Piaget in order to respond to this deficiency through the use of brevity while maintaining a degree of depth.

This approach has been successful in a curriculum effort whose goals were to take students to higher cognitive levels with maximum retention in a short period of time. It is recognized that the format used does not lend itself to smooth, flowing reading. The exposed concepts do make it possible for students to read the material clearly and briefly and enter into dialogue with the instructor.

The teaching goal is to set people free with theoretical knowledge of human growth, to provide opportunities for students to think, to write, to reason, and to apply concepts to life time experiences.

ERIK H. ERIKSON

Theory of Eight Stages
of Personality Development

ERIKSON: THE MAN AND HIS IDEAS

Erik H. Erikson presented his "Eight Stages of Man" to the White House Conference on Children in 1950. Today he is recognized as one of the most renowned psychologists and psychoanalysts in America. The recognition is well deserved; Erikson is a wise observer who notes universal patterns of feeling and attitude in personality development, especially in children and adolescents. He relates these insights to the whole life cycle. The splendor of his work is his ability to see through cultural limitations and perceive directly the essence of the human being.

Erikson was born of Danish parents in Frankfurt, Germany in 1902. His father abandoned his mother prior to his birth. His mother later married a pediatrician and they lived in Karlsrube, Germany during Erikson's early childhood. His adoptive father, Homberger, wanted the boy to become a pediatrician also. But Erikson's yearning for the arts and a wish to search out life on his own prompted him to drop out of high school. He left home as a young man with considerable talent but little direction.

He painted portraits of young children at play. At the age of twenty-five, a friend invited him to teach art in a small American experimental school in Vienna. It was a school for American children whose parents had come to Vienna to join the Freudian circle for psychoanalytic training and analysis. His schooling brought him in touch with Anna Freud and her emerging interest in psychoanalytical work with children. When Erikson became interested in her work, she accepted him as a student in psychoanalytic training and analysis. At this time in his life he was searching for a commitment. His experience with children in the psychoanalytic clinic with Anna Freud provided him the direction which he was to pursue for the rest of his life. He literally layed down the paint brush and picked up the pen for in his later life he painted a different kind of portrait: vivid pictures of the behavior, aspirations, disappointments of man throughout the life cycle.[26]

From 1927 to 1933, while in Vienna, Erikson completed his professional training in child psychoanalysis. He also completed a teaching certificate at the Montessori school. While in training with Anna Freud, he was exposed to Freudian psychology and psychoanalysis and was invited to participate in the Vienna Psychoanalytic society. This exposure had a tremendous intellectual impact. It influenced the research and writing he did throughout his life. Erikson was ambivalent about Freudian thought and could never feel comfortable about joining the traditional psychoanalytic movement. He felt stifled in not being able to express his own thoughts and explore his own methods. Later in life he was known to defend Freudian thought; he did not totally abandon his thinking but rather built on the Freudian foundation. He used Freud's theory as a beginning rather than an end. Freud presented man with a psychosexual theory; Erikson later emphasized the psychosocial development of man.[26]

While in Vienna, Erikson met and married Joan Monwat Serson., The threat of facism in Europe and an invitation from the Harvard Medical School in Boston brought the Eriksons to America. It became the adopted home of Erikson, his wife, Joan, two sons and a daughter. Erikson became a citizen of the United States in 1939. When asked if he enjoyed being a U.S. citizen he replied:

> One can become an American to some extent in one's own lifetime even if one started elsewhere. And once an American, one has to continue becoming an American.[15]

The first fifteen years in America Erikson worked on issues of human development that had caused much unrest in his own development. He did anthropological field studies with the Ogalala Sioux Indians of Pine Ridge, South Dakota, and also the Yurok Indians of Northern California.

He found personality syndromes he could not explain within the confines of traditional psychoanalytic theory. His observations led him to believe that not only did the Indian sense a break with the past, they could not identify with a future requiring the white man's cultural values.

He also studied and worked in a rehabilitation center for World War II shell-shocked veterans. Here the men had trouble reconciling their attitudes and feelings as soldiers with attitudes they had before the war. Erikson came to speak of the syndrome observed in both of these groups as one of identity confusion.

During this period, he also did extensive research on sex differences in children's play configuration as part of the longitudinal child development study at the University of California.

Over a decade later he summarized the implications of his life-time experiences, his clinical and anthropological observations in his first book, *Childhood and Society*. It was here he identified eight stages in the human life cycle, in each a new dimension of social interaction becomes possible. His first book appeared when he was forty-eight years old. Many have followed since.

Erikson applied his theory of the human life cycle to the study of historical figures. He chose men whose lives fascinated him, perhaps because he shared some affinity with their identity crisis. He chose to elaborate a particular crisis or episode in the individual's life which seemed to crystalize a life-theme that combined the activities of the past and gave direction to the future. His two best known historical biographies are *The Young Man Luther* and *Gandi's Truth*.

Erikson had a prestigious academic career in America: of researching, writing and teaching. He held academic and clinical appointments at many of the countries leading universities. He was affiliated with: Harvard Medical School, Yale University, The University of California, Menninger Foundation, The Austen Riggs Center, The University of Pittsburg, The Massachusetts Institute of Technolgy and Stanford University. Throughout his career he held two or three appointments simultaneously and traveled extensively.[31]

Maier noted that his academic accomplishments are most significant and most unusual considering he was a high school drop out with no formal academic career and only a Montessori teaching certificate.[26]

His writing career is equally impressive. Some of his best known books include: *Childhood and Society, Identity and the Life Cycle, Identity Youth and Crisis, Toys and Reasons, The Challenge of Youth, Gandi's Truth* and *The Young Man Luther*.

There is more and more teaching of Erikson's concepts in psychiatry, psychology, education and social work, in America and other parts of the world. His description of the stages of the life cycle are summarized in major textbooks. Clinicians are increasingly looking at their cases in Eriksonian terms; philosopher and theologians have acknowledged his importance.[8] His psychohistorical investigations have revitalized a field of study which has caught the interest of historians and political scientists alike.

Although Erikson's life-stages have an intuitive rightness about them, not everyone agrees totally with his formulations. Research investigators have found Erikson's theories somewhat difficult to test. This is not surprising inasmuch as Erikson's concepts take into account the infinite complexity of the human personality. As an artist, Erikson recognizes that there are many different ways to view the same phenomenon and a perspective that is congenial to one will not always be acceptable to another. He offers his stage description of the life cycle for those who find such perspectives agreeable and not as a world view that everyone should accept.[26]

ERIKSON'S BASIC THEORY OF
EIGHT STAGES OF PERSONALITY DEVELOPMENT

1. The growth of human development takes place in a sequence of stages.

2. One stage develops on top of another in space and in time. The stages form a hierarchy, not just a sequence.

3. In each stage of personality development throughout the life span, there is a central problem or a crisis that has to be solved temporarily, at least, if the person is to proceed with vigor and confidence to the next stage.

4. Each type of conflict or crisis appears in its purest form at a particular stage of development.

5. There is a polarity (pull between two poles) for each stage of development.

6. Health of personality is determined by the preponderance of a positive stage over a negative polarity.

7. Analysis of the stages is not determined by a strict dichotomy; it is not an all or nothing situation. Each individual has a measure of both poles.

Eight Stages of Personality Development

AGE	BASIC STAGE	POLARITY	VIRTUE
Infancy	Trust	Mistrust	Hope
Toddler	Autonomy	Doubt and Shame	Will Power
Pre-School	Initiative	Guilt	Purpose
Middle Years	Industry	Inferiority	Competence
Adolescence	Identity	Self-Diffusion	Fidelity
Young Adulthood	Intimacy	Isolation	Love
Adulthood	Generativity	Stagnation	Care
Aged	Ego Integrity	Despair	Wisdom

ERIKSON'S CONCEPTS OF DEVELOPMENT

According to Erikson, an individual has neither a set personality nor a set character structure. A person is always a personality in the making: developing and redeveloping. His theory is best understood from the perspective of the life cycle.

Stages of Development

1. The growth of human strength takes place in a sequence of stages.
2. The stages represent the patterned development of the various parts of a whole psychosocial personality.
3. Growth must take place not only step by step, but at a proper rate in a normal sequence.
4. In each stage of life a new strength is added to a widening ensemble and reintegrated at each stage in order to play its part in the full cycle.
5. In each stage, rudiments develop which seed growth essentials that appear in later stages.
6. The psychosocial developmental stages are the products of interactional experiences between each person and his world.
7. For each stage there is a designated polarity.
   a. The individual is pulled between opposite poles and incorporates opposites in order to create a new and unique life situation.
   b. The solution of the dilemma of each phase generates the struggle for the next developmental conquest.[16]

Epigenetic Theory

1. Erikson refers to his theory as an epigenetic diagram.
2. Epi means upon, and genesis means emergence.
3. One stage is built upon another and each must be integrated into the whole.
4. Anything that grows has a ground plan, and out of this plan the parts arise to form a functioning system.
5. Each vital personality part is systematically related to all others, and they all depend on the proper development in the proper sequence.

6. Each part exists in some form before its decisive and critical time arrives.

7. Each stage becomes a crisis with growth and awareness of a new part; there is a shift in instinctual energy which causes a specific vulnerability in that part.[16]

Crisis Theory

1. Every stage in the life cycle is marked by a specific psychosocial crisis.

2. The word crisis is used in a developmental sense to conote not a threat of catastrophe, but a turning point, a crucial period in which a decisive turn is unavoidable.

3. Psychosocial development proceeds by critical steps—moments of decision between progress and regression, integration and retardation.

4. The very process of growth provides new energy as society offers new and specific opportunities according to the cultural expectations of the phases of life.

Basic Stage

The term basic applies to an aspect of growth of the ego's strength that is neither a conscious process nor strictly unconscious. Neither the first components nor any of those that follow are especially conscious. All must exist from the beginning in some form.

Ego Strength

1. Erikson sees the ego as having a general balancing function, keeping systems in perspective and in readiness for action. The ego mediates between outer events and inner responses, between past and future, and between the higher and lower self.

2. The concept of ego strength accounts for the difference between feeling whole or fragmented, at best, establishing a sense of being at one with oneself as one grows and develops.

Virtues

1. When Erikson uses the term virtue, he uses the Latin meaning "adds to the spirit of men."

2. It is the *active* pervading quality of strength which is the essence of a strong ego.

3. Without the strengths of basic virtues, all other values and goodnesses lack vitality.[13]

4. The negative side of virtue is weakness, and the symptoms are disorder, dysfunction, disintegration, the particular rage which accumulates whenever man is hindered in perfection of virtue.

Culture

1. An individual's life course is decisively influenced by the era, area, and arrangements into which he or she is born.
2. Development is determined by chance or planned events—where, when, how and how much other people respond to the ever-developing individual.
3. Environment forces both limit and free the individual.
4. Culture can aggravate or downplay the developmental stages.
5. Culture can make the stages more or less intense and prolonged.

Note bibliography numbers 11, 12, 13, 15, 21, 26.

EIGHT STAGES OF PERSONALITY DEVELOPMENT

A Sense of Trust in Infancy

Trust Versus Mistrust

Virtue: Hope

After the baby spends a theoretic 266 days in the tranquility of the womb, the infant is literally pushed into a world full of startling conditions. As the nursery rhymes attest, for some it's a scary place to be. The period of total dependency called infancy is the time the child learns if the world is a good and satisfying place to live.[8] For the infant, the first year or so of social interaction will determine the degree of trust or mistrust and hope the child acquires to form the personality. Erikson believed that,

> This early interaction between mother and child builds a 'cradle of faith' and permits a mother to respond to the needs and demands of the baby's body and mind in a way that he learns once and for all to trust her, to trust himself, and to trust the world.[20]

A Sense of Trust, "I Am What I Am Given"

1. Infants who learn to trust:
   a. consistently and appropriately have their physical needs for nourishment, cleansing, sleep, warmth, and comfort filled. They are fed the right thing at the right time and in the right quantity.

7

b. are loved, cuddled, fondled, rocked, played with, and talked to. They are given the pleasure of love and dependency of love which is conveyed by the mother or significant caretaker's comforting warmth and quality care.[8]

c. are given a sense of predictability and sufficient trust to accept the unknown and unpredictable. They feel the world is a safe place to be and people are helpful and dependable. They have learned to rely on the sameness and continuity of routine.

d. are given the opportunity and encouragement to learn to trust their own bodies to do their bidding—to grasp for, to hold, to release, to roll over, to reach, to sit, and finally to stand. They are given the opportunity to learn how to give and receive, the basic rudiments of problem solving.

e. look forward to new experiences with favorable expectations. They grow psychologically as well as physically when they have learned to trust their world.

A Sense of Mistrust

1. Infants who learn to mistrust:
   a. are given inconsistent, inadequate, and rejecting care which fosters mistrust. They develop feelings of anxiety and uncertainty when needs are not met as they arise and discomforts are not eliminated.

   b. are taught an attitude of fear and suspicion toward the world in general and people in particular that carries through the later stages of development.

   c. are dealt a sense of uncertainty that results from a meager measure of love and all it implies. They do not develop normally physically, mentally, socially, or emotionally. It is a common finding that individuals diagnosed as "psychopathic personality" were so unloved in early infancy that they have no reason to trust the human race and, therefore, no sense of responsibility toward their fellow men.[34]

   d. are given unsatisfactory physical experiences and the frustration which is associated with them. They have a fearful apprehension of the environment and a lack of hope for change in trying anew.

   e. become irritable, demanding, and ever less lovable when needs are not adequately met. Infants may panic when gratification is distant and consistently delayed.

   f. may withdraw into themselves when at odds with themselves and others.

The Ratio of Trust to Mistrust

1. To learn to mistrust, according to Erikson, is also important. A certain ration of trust and mistrust in our basic social attitude is a critical factor.

2. When we enter a situation, we must determine how much we can trust and how much we can mistrust.[21] The ratio should be in favor of trust, tempered only with a small amount of mistrust. We need not consciously teach this; life has enough built-in situations in which we learn to mistrust.

Infants in Different Cultures

1. Mothers in different cultures, classes, and races teach trust in different ways so that it will fit their cultural version of the universe.[21]

2. In most primitive societies and in some sections of our own society, the attention accorded infants is more in line with natural processes. The scientific age has often produced nervous and self-conscious and insecure young mothers.

3. Cultural myths, superstitions, and historical trends often referred to as necessities and determine what is workable. Some infants are heavily swaddled, others are bound to cradle-boards, while others are rocked whenever they wimper.

4. Mothers who are given love and support from husbands, families, and society can in turn respond to all children with love and sensitive care.

5. Many cultures are gradually permitting men more participation in caring for the baby. According to Erikson, "Men will be better men for it."[20]

The Virtue: Hope

1. According to Erikson, a virtue is a quality, a basic human strength, something vital, needed for man to become humanly, morally strong. Hope is a very basic human virtue that is needed to stay alive.

2. The rudiments of hope rely on the infant's needs being filled with love and appropriate care.

3. Spitz's studies show that children who give up hope because they do not get enough loving and enough stimulation may literally die.[32]

4. According to Erikson, it would be difficult to specify the criteria for hope and harder yet to measure it. Yet, he who has seen a hopeless child knows what is not there.[22]

5. The gradual widening at each step of the infant's experiences provides verification of life which inspires new hopefulness. Because of man's lifelong struggles between trust and mistrust in changing conditions, hope has to develop firmly, and then be confirmed and reaffirmed throughout life.[21]

6. The first stage for man is the development of hope emanating from a favorable ratio of trust to mistrust.

A Sense of Autonomy in Toddlerhood

Autonomy Versus Shame and Doubt
Virtue: Willpower

Once the sense of trust is firmly established, the struggle for the next component of the healthy personality begins. Only when toddlers have trust, do they dare to respond with confidence to their newly felt desire to assert themselves boldly. They discover that they can determine their own behavior, and with it acquire a sense of autonomy. The child moves rapidly away from almost total dependence of babyhood toward young childhood and becomes aware of himself as a person.

The child's sense that he is an independent, autonomous human being, and yet one who is able to use the help and guidance of others, is at stake throughout the struggle of these years. This stage of development becomes decisive in the significance of the ratio between love and hate—cooperation and willfulness—freedom of self expression and its renunciation in the makeup of the individual.[16,17]

A Sense of Autonomy, "I Am What I Will"

1. Autonomy builds upon the child's new mental and motor abilities which lend themselves to the mastery of his own body. The toddler can now: walk, trot, climb up and down, open, close, drop, push, and manipulate objects in ever more complicated ways.

2. This is a period of muscle-system maturation and the consequent ability (and doubly felt inability) to coordinate a number of highly conflicting action patterns such as those of the modalities: 1) to hold onto and to let go; 2) to withhold and to expel; 3) to seize and to drop; and 4) to handle and to explore.[11]

3. The training of the eliminative sphincters can become the center of the struggle over inner and outer control. If the parents usurp control over the child's organic functions, it can lead to a needless but potentially damaging battle of wills. If the child loses, shame can result.[33]

4. This is the period when the child needs to build the concept that his body is his friend. Toddlers are willing to practice over and again skills that will enhance their independence.

5. For toddlers to develop their sense of autonomy, it is necessary they experience (again and again) that they are people who are permitted to make choices. Decisions are often made in the forceful form of "No," "Mine," or the use of "body language."

6. Toddlers are curious, and as they develop autonomy, they explore their world and in the process tip over, spill, drop, pull out, shove, and take away from.

7. At the time the toddler is becoming autonomous, he must learn some of the boundaries of self-determination. He inevitably finds that there are walls he cannot climb, and objects he is not permitted to touch.

8. Individual styles, tempos, and temperament characterize the toddler's thrust for independence. Some toddlers are bold, some are timid; some are rough, and others gentle. Independence comes in many forms.

9. Toddler behavior is sometimes a frightening and frustrating period for parents who do not understand the desire to be autonomous. Yet the adult must back the toddler in his wish to "stand on his own feet," lest he be overcome by shame that he has exposed himself foolishly and by doubt in his self-worth.[23]

10. From a sense of self-control without loss of self-esteem comes a healthy sense of autonomy and pride.[23]

Shame and Doubt

1. Shame and doubt are emotions some parents use to control children. It exhibits the child's sense of being small. According to Erikson, those who guide the growing child wisely avoid shaming him and avoid causing him to doubt that he is a person of worth. Shaming exploits an increasing sense of dependence; it makes one self-conscious. One is visible and not ready to be visible.[23]

2. Parents need to be firm but tolerant and loving with the toddler so that he can rejoice in being a person of independence and can grant independence to others. Erikson believes that a child's sense of autonomy is a reflection of his parents' personal dignity.

3. A toddler's development of autonomy, or shame, or doubt, depends to a great extent upon the caring person's capacity to grant gradual independence to the child. Parents need to feel comfortable with themselves and comfortable in granting freedom in increasing areas while maintaining firmness in others. This give and take between child and caring people is reflected in the child's sense of self-assurance.

4. A person probably never develops without any shame or embarrassment, and limited amounts appear to cause no permanent damage. Shame is expressed in many cultures in terms of "losing face," a most terrible experience. In American culture shame is expressed in such honest statements as, "I wish the floor would open up so I could fall through."

5. In considering the polarity, Erikson is not saying that autonomy should be produced and the other not at all. Both must emerge out of this developmental stage. The ratio, according to Erikson, should be in favor of autonomy. One who has more shame than autonomy will feel and act inferior all his life—or consistently be counteracting that feeling.[21]

6. If denied the gradual and well guided experience of the autonomy, of free choice, the child may withdraw, stop trying, sneak, or learn to manipulate.

7. When caretakers are impatient and do for the child what he is capable of doing for himself, they reinforce a sense of doubt. When they are harsh and criticize "accidents," the child develops an excessive sense of shame and doubts his ability to control his world and himself.

8. There is evidence that toddlers are the most abused children in our society. It is difficult to believe that the toddler's struggle for autonomy can be so threatening and misunderstood that it can elicit this type of punishment from threatened and angry parents.

9. Much of the shame and doubt, much of the indignity and uncertainty aroused in children is a consequence of the parents' frustrations in marriage, in work, and in citizenship.[12]

10. The degree and type of behavior permitted the child, and the way in which the control of his behavior is handled bears upon the child's attitude toward himself, toward social organizations, and ideals later in life.[26]

The Virtue: Willpower

1. The virtue to be developed in this stage is willpower, a natural outgrowth of autonomy. As the toddler faces the double demand for self-control and for the acceptance of the control of others, he often pits his will against the will of his caretakers. Erikson calls this warfare of unequal wills, for often the child is unequal to his own violent drives, and the parent and child are unequal to each other.[16]

2. Making decisions is part of the evaluative quality inherent in being alive; ego strength depends on seeing one's self as having worth. According to Erikson, no person can live and no ego can remain intact without hope and willpower.[24]

3. Parents can demonstrate that good will arises from a mutual limitation of will. Cooperation gradually grants a liberating measure of self-control to the child who starts to control willfulness and to train his willingness.[24]

4. Only the rudiments of willpower develop at this level. Without this development of fundamental willpower, the future mature human capacity cannot develop.

5. This is the stage in which the child must develop the autonomy and willpower "to be his own person." The toddler's struggle for autonomy forms the foundation for adolescent independence.

A Sense of Initiative in Preschool

Initiative Versus Guilt

Virtue: Purpose

According to Erikson:

> There is in every child at every stage a new miracle of vigorous unfolding which constitutes a new hope and a new responsibility for all. Such is the sense and pervading quality of *initiative*.

> The child suddenly seems to grow together, both in his person and in his body. He appears "more himself: more loving, relaxed, and brighter in his judgement and more activated and more activating."

> He is in free possession of a sense of energy which permits him to forget failures quickly and to approach what seems desirable with more accurate direction.[23]

A Sense of Initiative, "I Am What I Imagine I Will Be"

1. This is a period of enterprise and imagination, an emulative, creative period when fantasy substitutes for literal execution of desires, and the most meager equipment provides material for high imaginings.

2. It is a period in which the child can put his plans and ideas into action. Both language and locomotion permit him to expand his understanding, imagination and activity.

3. It is a period of intrusion:

    a. into other people's bodies by physical force.

    b. into other people's ears and minds by loud, aggressive talking.

    c. into space by vigorous locomotion.

    d. into the unknown by consuming curiosity.[11]

4. It is a period in which preschool children:

    a. have a boundless supply of energy and are in mastery of their bodies: can walk, climb, skip, run, ride a tricycle, etcetera.

    b. find pleasurable accomplishment in wielding and manipulating the tools and toys of their culture in ever more complicated ways.

    c. make replicas of the world around them and use the intricate structures in dramatic play.

    d. initiate motor activities on their own and no longer merely respond to or imitate the actions of other children or adults.[8]

    e. invest time in refining muscular activities, accuracy in perception, and skills in communication.

    f. are ready to mature in a sense of sharing obligations.

5. Children this age:

    a. identify with responsible and caring adults who provide them with a constructive outlet for initiative and set the stage for future responsibility.

    b. need opportunities to explore, to act, to do, and to create. They are better planners and starters than they are finishers. The ability to initiate plans and take action enhances their feeling of pride in accomplishment and helps them to become self-starters.

    c. run in terror in nightmares and dreams from fantasies of monsters and lions and fears of losing some part of their body.

d. observe with keen attention and imitate what interesting grown-ups do (their parents, the paramedics, nurses, doctors) and yearn for a share in their activity.

e. become more interested in having friends. Their plans and ideas are often initiated as cooperative endeavors with others.

6. Rudiments of parent-like behavior can be observed as children this age start supervising themselves and others in reality and in play situations.

7. Children need parents and teachers who value play. According to Erikson:

a. Play is a way of life for a child and a prime necessity for healthy growth. It helps the child's ego deal with reality.

b. Play is to the child what thinking and planning are to the adult.

c. Play provides a trial universe in which conditions are simplified and consequences of failure are less severe.

d. Play offers a child a time to learn to trust himself and to trust others; a time to practice being independent and autonomous, and an opportunity to initiate plans and ideas.

8. Erikson feels that initiative is a necessary part of every act, and man needs a sense of initiative for whatever he learns and does. Just as Americans prize autonomy, so, too, do they prize initiative.[28]

9. If, during the preschool period, the child can get some sense of the various roles he can perform as an adult, he will be ready to progress joyfully to the next stage where he will find pleasurable accomplishment in activities less filled with fantasy.

A Sense of Guilt

1. By this age, the conscience has developed. The child is no longer guided only by the outsider; there is instilled within him a voice or knowing that comments on his deeds and judges and warns. Children now begin to feel guilty for mere thought, for deeds that have been imagined but never executed.

a. The conscience is built from the model of the caring person.

b. Children will incorporate into their conscience what the parent or caring person is as a person and not merely what he or she tries to teach the child.[18]

2. The problem to be worked out in this stage of development for the child is how to will without too great a sense of guilt (transgression of parental values). Failure to work through will leave the personality overburdened and possibly over-restricted by guilt.

3. The child may be made to feel that his motor activity is bad; his imaginative play is silly and stupid; his distortion of reality is a lie; his fears and phobias are a nuisance; and his exploration of his body and language is offensive. Just as some parents use shame and doubt to control, some parents now add the burden of guilt.

4. It is easy to see how the child's developing sense of initiative may be discouraged. Many of the projects dreamed up at this age are of a kind which cannot be permitted because they are impossible to execute. Initiative may be thwarted as soon as the practical meets the ideal. On the other hand, initiative must foster so the preschool child becomes the creative adult.

5. When the fondest hopes and wildest fantasies are continually repressed and inhibited, an inner powerhouse of rage within the child must be submerged.[23] These restrictions may cause the child to unconsciously incorporate resentment, bitterness, and vindictive attitudes toward the world into functioning parts of his personality.

6. The child is experiencing himself as more powerful than ever before; and, on the other hand, he is beginning to realize that he must control his own behavior and that he will feel guilty if he fails to do so.

7. A polarity of initiative versus either passivity or guilt for having gone too far—that is, living too strongly or too weakly compared to their inner strivings—provides the major theme of this period.

The Virtue: Purpose

1. The particular virtue Erikson sees coming from initiative is "purpose."

2. Out of the initiative develops goal-directedness for the individual. The child begins to envision goals for which his locomotion and cognition have prepared him. He begins to have projects and sees that the kind of person he wants to be involves being able to do particular kinds of things.

3. A child begins to learn that he must work for things. He becomes aware of society's institutions and of the opportunities and roles which require responsible participation when he becomes an adult.[26]

4. Erikson implies that the individual's potential capacity to work and achieve economic success within the framework of society's economic order depends upon his or her mastery of this period.

5. A child's ability to leave this stage with a sense of initiative and purpose out-balancing his sense of guilt depends to a considerable degree upon how the parents and teachers respond to his self-initiated activities.

A Sense of Industry in Middle Years of Childhood

Industry Versus Inferiority
Virtue: Competence

Personality at the first stage crystallizes around the conviction, "I am what I am given;" and that of the second, "I am what I will;" and the third can be characterized by, "I am what I can imagine I will be." The fourth stage is this: "I am what I can learn." To the degree that a sense of trust, a sense of autonomy, and a sense of initiative have been achieved, the school years child is now prepared to move into the sense of industry. The word industry, according to Erikson, means being busy with something, learning to complete something, doing a job. In each of these periods a child becomes a very different person, a person with increased cognitive capacities, with increased physical skills, and increased ability to interact with a wider range of people in whom he is interested, who understand him, and who react to him.

It is as if a middle-years child knows that he is psychologically ready and must now become a worker. He learns to win recognition in the stage of industry by producing things. He develops a sense of pleasure in mastering and using skills of the culture and by assuming more adult-like responsibility. The danger of the period is that a child may find himself lacking and feel inadequate and inferior as he tries to develop the talents thought necessary to become competent.[28]

A Sense of Industry, "I Am What I Can Learn"

1. For middle-years children these are the skill-building years. They are also the game-playing years.

2. This is a period in which middle-years children learn to use both the tools and toys of their particular culture and master the skills that are considered most important by the group.

17

a. The Eskimo child will learn to use a net, a spear, and a gun for hunting and fishing.

b. A child from the islands of the South Pacific will learn to paddle adroitly and maneuver a canoe.

c. Children living on farms will learn to use the equipment of farming and acquire skill needed for caring for animals.

d. In a highly technological society, children will acquire mathematical, reading, and writing skills for advancement in society.[1]

3. Children, after a period characterized by exuberant imagination, want to learn how to do things and how to do them well.

a. Children are concerned with how things are made and how they work.

b. Children want to be engaged in real tasks that can be carried through to completion.

c. Children learn the value of work, cooperation, and responsibility.

d. Children develop attitudes and habits toward work that will make productive members of society.

e. Children learn the fundamentals of technology and use the skills to perform according to expectations.

f. Children strive to master the basic motor, social, and intellectual skills they need to get along.

4. Ideally, a child develops a sense of industry as one strong component of personality. However, Erikson says a child may over-react and value utilitarianism too much. If the child accepts work as his only obligation and "what works" as the only criterion of worthwhileness, the child may become a confirming and thoughtless slave of the technology and of those who are in a position to exploit him.[9]

5. A child in every culture receives some systematic instruction.

a. In preliterate societies, much is learned from adults and older children who become teachers by acclamation rather than by appointment. Knowledge gained is related to the basic skills of simple technology which can be understood as the child gradually handles the utensils, the tools, and the weapons used by big people.[23]

b. More literate people with more specialized careers must prepare the child by teaching things which first make him literate. A child is given the widest possible basic education for the greatest number of possible career choices.[23]

6. A child this age needs some degree of success to develop a sense of industry—a feeling that he can cope with the challenges encountered. He needs encouragement and praise so that the sense of industry can be enhanced.

7. Teachers are in a unique position to maximize a student's achievements and feelings of competence by encouraging or rewarding efforts, stimulating interest in learning, and minimizing failures and limitations.

8. Children readily identify with parent's attitude toward school and education. Thus, parents who value and speak highly of school foster more positive values than do parents whose words or actions show that they attach little importance to it.[7]

9. The world of peers assumes an equally important position. Children's attitudes are influenced by how good they are at activities that are valued by their peers.

10. It is in this period that children acquire not only knowledge and skill for good workmanship, but also the ability to cooperate and play fair and follow the rules of social games.

11. Under reasonably favorable circumstances, this is a period of calm, steady growth.

A Sense of Inferiority

1. The chief danger of this period is the presence of conditions that may lead to the development of a sense of inadequacy. If the child experiences more failure than success, he is likely to develop a sense of inferiority—a feeling that he is incapable of meeting the challenges of the world.[7] Inferiority may be the outcome if the child has not yet achieved the capacity to initiate, or his experiences at home have not prepared him for school.

2. Feelings of lack of worth and inadequacy come from two sources: from self and from the picture flashed back from others in the social environment. When the reward structure in society is so keenly attuned to evidence of mastery, a child who is not capable of developing skills must surely experience heightened feelings of inferiority.[28]

3. If a child has a chronic disability or does not have the aptitude, preference, or capability for specific skills, the inevitable result will be feelings of inadequacy. A few failure experiences can generate such strong negative feelings that the child will avoid engaging in new tasks in order to avoid failure.[28]

4. When a child is made to feel that the color of his skin, the background of his parents, or the fashion of his clothes rather than the wish and will to learn will decide his worth, he begins to feel inferior in an insensitive, shallow society.[9]

5. Too often one sees the reluctance, the self-doubt, and the withdrawal of a child who feels extremely inferior. To resolve the crisis in the direction of inferiority suggests that this child cannot conceive of the potential to contribute to the welfare of the large community.

6. Middle-school age children are often shamed for failure, just as toddlers are shamed for inability to control body functions. The earlier themes of doubt and guilt are intimately associated with feelings of inferiority.

7. If the child continuously fails to meet the standards set by adults, parents, school, and peers, there is no alternative but to incorporate into the personality a view of oneself as a failure.

Virtue: Competence

1. Competence comes from knowing that most of the time one can acceptably, adequately, surely, unquestionably accomplish a given task, skill, or activity.

2. A sense of accomplishment comes from having done well among one's peers, parents, family, and teachers.

3. In work, at school, at play, and at home there are many opportunities for a child to get a feeling of mastery and worthwhile endeavor.

4. The schools are the legally constituted arrangement for giving instruction to the young, so the professional responsibility rests on the teacher for helping all children achieve a sense of industry and a feeling of competence in their society.

5. The selection and training of teachers is vital for the avoidance of the dangers which can befall the individual at this stage. The development of a sense of inferiority, the feeling that one will never be "any good," is a danger which can be minimized by a teacher who knows how to emphasize what a child *can* do.[13]

6. Neither teachers nor parents can work alone. Jointly they can do much, not only for children of healthy personalities but also for many whose development has been handicapped.

7. The rudiments of skill add method to hope, will, and purpose. Thus, workmanship and accomplishment which come from convincing experience, prepare in the child a future sense of competency without which there can be no strong ego.[24]

A Sense of Identity in Adolescents

Identity Versus Role Diffusion
Virtue: Fidelity

Identity is an integration of all previous identifications and self images. According to Erikson, it begins when the child first recognizes his mother, when her voice tells him he is somebody with a name, and that he's good.[21] He has to go through many stages before he reaches the identity that emerges from a successfully accomplished adolescent period. His identity is built on his ability to trust himself and others. Adolescent independence is built on the rudiments of willpower and autonomy that develop in the toddler stage. The initiative of the preschool child emerges in the form of curiosity and experimentation with different roles. Industry forms the foundation for a sense of duty and a feeling of workmanship. But self-image is based on both positive and negative identity. The negative is composed of the lack of trust, the experiences in shame and guilt, and the failures in competency and goodness.

A sense of identity implies a mastery of the problems of childhood and a genuine readiness to face, as a potential equal, the challenges of the adult world. The adolescent seeks to clarify who he is, what his role in society is to be. Youth asks the question, "Which way can I be?" He seldom inquires, "Who am I?" because his identity depends upon his becoming his identity.[23]

A Sense of Identity: "I Am What I Can Accept To Become"

1. According to Erikson, adolescents are in a transitional period between childhood and adulthood.
   a. The adolescent is confronted with a host of psychological, physiological, sexual, and cognitive changes, as well as new and varied intellectual, social, and vocational demands.
   b. The adolescent is asserting autonomy and demanding independence. Emotion is often volatile; control is often inadequate.
   c. The adolescent is self-consciously trying on different roles in hope of finding one which seems to "fit."
   d. The adolescent tends to be uncompromising in his prejudices and belligerently loyal to his own group's ideas and values.

e. The adolescent tends to see experimentation as critical. Interest in extremes; experiments with opposites, especially those frowned upon by elders, become the center of role experimentation with his self-image.

f. The adolescent finds being against something fills one of his greatest needs, for through contrasting himself and his ideas with an opposite group's, he defines his sense of self.[14]

2. Youth has the intellectual capacity to think of many variables and alternatives which aid in the search for an individual identity but, at the same time, increase the difficulty of the search. The adolescent is concerned about these things:

   a. the unsettled question of vocational identity and economic status. He assesses his liabilities and assets and how he wants to use them.

   b. finding those to love and to like, and finding those who also love and like him.

   c. coming to grips with a personal philosophy: moral, religious, political values and standards which assume special prominence and are vital to the development of a strong sense of identity.

3. An adolescent may arrive at a positive identity choice through the negative process of elimination. The negative options often detemine a positive direction. One day at hard, physical labor may inspire an individual to return to school to become a journeyman apprentice.

Peers and a Sense of Identity

1. Adolescents of this stage of development are easily influenced by the attitudes of others, particularly the peer group. The importance of peers in the process of finding out "Who am I?" cannot be over-emphasized.

2. Since an identity can be found only through interaction with other people, the adolescent goes through a period of compulsive peer group conformity as a means of testing roles to see how they fit him.

3. Belonging to a peer group, in-group, or gang conveys the impression that a final solid identity has been achieved in the subculture, when actually, it is only a temporary, tryout sort of identity that the group has generated and decorated with the fads of the day.

4. Peer groups provide an individual with both a role model and direct feedback about himself. The security that the peer group provides remains strong, and the ensuing disapproval and intolerance of "differences," including petty aspects of language, gesture, hair style, and dress,

is explained by Erikson as the "necessary defense," a temporary identity against the dangers of self diffusion that exist between childhood and adult status.

5. Adolescents need to experience a degree of comfort in the range of contacts with the opposite sex. Erikson suggests that the teenager's first few serious exposures to "falling in love" have perhaps more to do with self-discovery than with sexuality. Long hours of conversation and telephone dialogue provide the opportunity to explore identities together.[25]

6. Adolescent love is often an attempt to test one's own diffused ego through the eyes of a beloved person in order to clarify and reflect one's own self concept and one's ego identity.

7. Eventually, individuals have to free themselves from this peer group orientation in order to become themselves.

Parents and a Sense of Identity

1. For the adolescent, the family framework is too limited to try out new images and roles. The adolescent often rebels against parental dominance, their value system, and parent's intrusion into their private life since they must separate their own identity from that of their family. They must establish and, if need be, demand their autonomy to reach maturity.

2. If decision-making is not allowed within the family system, the adolescent will be ill-equipped as an adult to direct his energies and talents toward worthwhile goals.

3. Parental limits on the adolescent thrust for independence must be decreased by degree when the adolescent shows the desire and the ability to assume responsibility for his own actions.

4. Parents go through an identity crisis of their own at this time. In order to remain friends with their adolescent, they must be willing to accept the "identity their adolescent chooses to become." This is not an easy task.

Education and the Sense of Identity

1. Schools often require adolescents to submit and suppress their creativity, individuality, and identity to the demands of the skill-and-knowledge oriented curriculum in order for the schools to succeed.

2. Education systems seem to be encouraging foreclosure, since they demand conformity to the way things are and submission to authority, rather than aiding the adolescent in his search for a unique individuality and a personal identity.[25]

1. Patterns of identity formation may vary widely among adolescents as a result of many influences, ranging from parent-child relations to cultural or subcultural pressures to the rate of social change.

2. Within a particular society, identities may be typical or deviant. The individual may seek personal, social, and vocational roles that are expected and approved by society or, in contrast, he or she may seek more idiosyncratic roles which may be negative.[4]

3. In more primitive cultures there are pubery rites which rather forcefully inform the growing youth where he/she belongs, and that he/she must pay the price of conformity for a sense of belongingness to a particular tribe or a particular clan.[21]

4. The more free choice and decision a culture gives as to whom one is going to be, the more difficult the identity conflict is to resolve.

5. James Marcia has expanded Erikson's theory of identity versus role diffusion by identifying four patterns of identity status.[27]

   a. *The identity diffused* or identity confused subject has not yet experienced an identity crisis, nor has he made any commitment to a vocation or to a set of beliefs. The individual does not know who he is, where he is going, or who he wants to become.

   b. *The foreclosure subject* has accepted the values and commitments of others, especially parents, without exploring and actively searching for alternatives.

   c. *The moratorium subject* is in an acute state of crisis; he is exploring and actively searching for alternatives; he is struggling to find his identity from a variety of alternatives.

   d. *The identity achieved* subject has experienced crises; but has resolved the problems in his own terms and made personal commitments to an occupation, a religious belief, a personal value system.

Marcia believes that the moratorium appears to be an essential prerequisite for identity achievement since identity cannot be achieved without searching and exploring. He believes there is danger in the blind acceptance in the foreclosure status. The person can never attain a true identity achieved status unless that identity is truely his own.[22]

A Sense of Role Diffusion

1. According to Erikson, at no other phase of the life cycle is the promise of finding oneself and the threat of losing oneself so closely allied.[19]

2. Identity is not given to the individual by society, nor does it appear as a maturational phenomenon, like pubic hair; it must be acquired through sustained individual effort. Unwillingness to work on one's own identity formation carries with it the danger of role diffusion.[27]

3. The identity confused adolescent may do these things:

   a. sport an identity confusion very openly and almost mockingly, for he may prefer to find his own way to new ethical commitments rather than embrace those already established.[21]

   b. run away in one form or another by dropping out of school, leaving home or job, staying out all night, or exhibiting bizarre behavior.

   c. completely lose his individuality by over-identifying with the heroes of cliques and crowds.[13]

   d. take pride in being delinquent, ornery, and reactionary. The cultural majority may unwittingly encourage and confirm this behavior by tagging him with names such as dropout, long hair, hippie, or junkie.[21]

4. It sometimes appears as if a delinquent youngster, in rebelling against the conformist pressure of conventional society, has become a conformist in a delinquent subculture. It's possible an escape to this "deviant subculture" from conformist demands is not an escape from conformity at all.[21]

5. Erikson maintains that too often adults fail to see that the delinquent adolescent is looking for the chance to conform to some subculture, to be loyal to some leader, and to display some kind of fidelity or faithfulness.[4]

6. The adolescent may begin (consciously or unconsciously) to recognize his own negative identity in his parents and begin to doubt whether earlier identifications with them are altogether as useful and admirable as previously thought.

7. He may start to use psychological crutches to rationalize his behavior. He becomes proud of his neuroses, or blames everything on his childhood or his parents or social conditions.

8. Adolescent cognitive capacities and social interests are such that they want to go to the limit of experience before they fit themselves into their culture and fit their culture to themselves.

The Virtue: Fidelity

1. Fidelity is the capacity to be faithful. According to Erikson, when one reaches a certain age, one can and must learn to be faithful to some ideological view.

2. Adolescents are looking for significant adults and ideas in whose service they can prove themselves trustworthy.

3. They are searching for a commitment to specific roles selected from many alternatives, and they must make a series of ever-narrowing selections of personal, occupational, sexual, and ideological commitments.

4. They are striving for self-direction which becomes a major force in the preservation of identity. Striving for independence, combined with the anticipation of approaching adulthood, makes the adolescent weigh carefully his behavior, abilities, and weaknesses with the future in mind. They search for long-term meanings and goals and decide what kind of people they want to be.[14]

5. Without the development of a capacity for fidelity, the individual will either have what is called a weak ego, or look for a deviant group to be faithful to.

6. Adolescents and those who have not matured beyond the adolescent stage are easily seduced by totalitarian regimes and all kinds of totalistic fads which offer some transitory fake values.[14]

7. Erikson believes that limited fidelity expands to universal fidelity to form a wider identity and should become a thrust for all mankind.

8. Adolescents find their identity as they blend from adolescence into adulthood. They are aware of their progressive continuity between what they have come to be, during the long years of childhood, and what they promise to become in the anticipated future.

9. Self-concept vacillates between what they conceive themselves to be and what they perceive others to see in them and expect of them.

10. Adolescence is thus a vital regenerator in the process of social evolution; for youth selectively offers its loyalties and energies to the conservation of what feels true to them and to the correction or destruction of that which does not seem right to them.[24]

A Sense of Intimacy for the Young Adult

Intimacy Versus Isolation
Virtue: Love

With childhood and youth at an end, the individual begins life as a full member in our western society. It is the time for the young adult to settle seriously to the task of full participation in the community. It is a time to enjoy life with adult liberty and adult responsibility. It is a time to nurture a spouse and children. It is a time to develop togetherness for family.

According to Erikson:

> It is only after a reasonable sense of identity has been established that real intimacy with the other sex (or, for that matter, with any other person or even with oneself) is possible. The youth who is not sure of his identity shies away from interpersonal intimacy, but the surer he becomes of himself, the more he seeks it in the form of friendship, leadership, love, and inspiration.[11]

A Sense of Intimacy, "I Am What I Can Give," or "We Are What We Can Love"

1. The person who has resolved the major identity question of adolescence is ready for deeper, more intimate relationships with others. A relationship that is truly personal, an in-depth opening up and sharing, depends on having attained a firm sense of one's own self.[13] Success or failure no longer depends directly upon the parents, but only indirectly as they have contributed to the individual's success or failure at earlier stages.

2. Friendship, love, sexual intimacy, even intimacy with oneself, one's inner resources, the range of one's excitement and commitments are examples of moving beyond identity. Expressions of vulnerability and inadequacy can be made intrust to the intimate partner without fear of rejection.

3. The achievement of psychological adulthood entails these tasks:

   a. continued growth and time devoted to study or to work at a specified career.

   b. social intercourse with the other sex in order to select a partner for the extended intimate relationship of marriage.

   c. a broader, more flexible outlook, a greater sense of security with other people, a less narcissistic (bound-to-the-self) conception of what is desirable and what is possible in life.

27

d. the capacity to develop a true psychosocial intimacy with another person, be it friendship or love.

   e. progression from emotional dependence on parents and peers to relative autonomy.

4. The eighteen-year-old who took some questionable social cause seriously enough to risk disapproval may, only a decade later, be a pillar of community respectability.

5. The young adult capable of intimacy is self-aware, self-accepting, independent, and trusting. Tenderness, openess, and vulnerability are seen as appropriate qualities in mature men and women.[6] Ideally, intimacy replaces parental love; equal partnership supplements domination and obedience.

Marriage, Children, and the Sense of Intimacy

1. When Erikson speaks of intimacy he means much more than lovemaking. He means the ability to share with and care about another person without fear of losing oneself in the process.

2. Healthy young adults accept and celebrate the sexual desire they feel for and evoke in others.[6] Erikson states that sexual intimacy is only part of what he has in mind. It is obvious that sexual intimacies do not always wait for the ability to develop a true and mutual psychological intimacy with another person.[11]

3. Many young peole marry today hoping to find themselves by finding one another. But the early obligations and responsibilities as workers, mates, and parents disrupt the completion of their own identity.[12] Studies of sociologist reveal that:

    a. early marriages characteristically are not as stable as are marriages between more mature people.

    b. if marriage is begun before one or both partners have established an identity, the chances for a happy, lasting marriage are low, and divorce statistics are extremely high.

4. Tremendous support can be found for Erikson's belief that one needs an answer to the question, "Who am I?" before one can select a person with whom to live the rest of his life. "The giving of oneself to another, which is the mark of true intimacy, cannot occur until one has a self to give."[5]

5. Intimacy implies that one is ready and has the ability and willingness to share mutual trust, to regulate cycles of work procreation, and recreation for each partner's fullest and most self-satisfying partipation in society, to prepare a foundation for the healthy development of their offspring.[26]

6. Those people who do not choose to become parents develop through this experience by contributing to the care of societies' children.

7. The women's liberation movement, the Equal Rights Ammendment, and changing life styles have tempered Erikson's earlier position on intimacy and the identity crisis. He originally felt that women had to keep their identities incomplete until they selected a partner. He now recognizes that his theory functions within an historical context, and women are establishing identity within marriage and without marriage, with children and without children, and within careers formerly dominated by men.

A Sense of Isolation

According to Erikson:

1. The counterpart of intimacy is isolation: the readiness to repudiate, isolate, and, if necessary, destroy those forces and people whose essence seems dangerous to one's own.[23]

2. One is afraid to take chances with one's identity by sharing true intimacy. Such inhibition is often reinforced by a fear of the outcome of intimacy: rejection and more isolation.

3. Excessive self-love and the inability to give of self are not only signs of emotional immaturity but also of a personality disorder—one who is incapable of this emotional giving is going to have grave difficulties in adjusting to marriage.[30]

4. When a youth does not accomplish intimate relationships with others or develop inner resources in early adulthood, he may settle for highly stereotyped interpersonal relationships and come to retain a deep sense of isolation and self-absorption.

5. The individual who is a prisoner of self, who is still occupied with an adolescent-type search for selfhood, is not up to full appreciation of other selves, and faces extreme difficulty in performing in the role as husband and father or wife and mother.

6. Too strong an attachment to one or both parents will create severe problems, especially in marital adjustment.

7. The young adult who is dependent on his peers, as he was on his parents, is far from being emotionally mature and would see the need for greater maturity before entering into lasting commitments.

8. There are partnerships which amount to an isolation, protecting both partners from the necessity to face the next critical development—that of generativity.[23]

The Virtue: Love

1. "We are what we love," is significant for the plural pronoun, "We." Rather than "I," it is a reflection of the intimacy of the relationship.

2. "We are what we can give" implies the readiness to nurture the development of others and implies the ability to put others, spouse, and children, before self.

3. Mature love relationships flower when a person has become secure enough to appreciate others on their own terms. This does not mean that adolescents necessarily lack meaningful personal relationships. Rather, it indicates that there is an even more mature level of love and concern. A person grows after the developmental personality needs of adolescence have been met.

4. Graduation from adolescence requires a sense of identity; graduation from the first phase of adulthood requires finding a sense of shared identity.

5. The solidarity of marriage is an evolutionary and individual achievement of the selectivity of mature love—the mutual verification through an experience of finding oneself, as one loses oneself in another.

6. The young adult achieves a personalized pattern of living which fosters an "individual identity within joint intimacy." He or she is able to merge their identity with another without losing their own identity.[23]

7. Sexual intimacy, genuine friendship, stable love, and successful marriage are the positive outcome of developed intimacy. Marriage, a young family, a career, and accepted responsibility as a citizen are the positive outcome of developed intimacy.

8. It is important to realize that only graduation from adolescence permits the development of that intimacy, that selflessness of joined devotion which anchors love in a mutual commitment.[24]

A Sense of Generativity in Adulthood

Generativity Versus Stagnation
Virtue: Care

Generativity stems from all the virtues and wisdom a person has accumulated. Erikson defines it as the "concern in establishing, guiding, and passing on the skills and values of one's culture to the next generation."[9] This responsibility needs to be shared by virtually all adults and all institutions in society, such as church, schools, community, and industry."

The individual is now presumably ready to take his place in society at large and aid in the development and perfection of whatever his/her generation has produced. People must go beyond the few intimate relationships established in young adulthood—with spouse, children, close friends, and family—and become concerned with the next generation, with humanity in a broad sense.

A Sense of Generativity, "I Am What I Help Create"

1. Generativity means everything that is generated from generation to generation: children, ideas, works of art, and service to fellow man for the ongoing progress of the human species.[21]

2. People need not have children themselves in order for the generative impulse to flourish. Generativity can emerge from productivity and creativity in various areas. It is important to note that having children does not necessarily guarantee generativity.[29]

3. A person can "generate" by making a commitment and a contribution appropriate to his/her particular potential and competency; a good mother, a good janitor, a good scout leader, are examples of exhibiting generativity.

4. With the world's plan for population control, it is important for us to support the idea that a person can be generative by helping to create a world that can promise an acceptable and positive mimimum to every child born.

5. A sense of generativity within an individual includes parental responsibility for society's family efforts and interests in supporting measures for child care, education, the arts and sciences, all traditions which soon will enter into the newly developing individual's life span.[6]

6. Personal and creative life merge with community life. These should become one, or self-absorption can drain and estrange a person's efforts for the community.

7. Erikson sees the contact with young people—as supportive mentor or director or co-worker—as a significant part of middle age. If middle-aged people withdraw and do not become a part of the world in which young people live, they are likely to become stagnant, self-absorbed, and unhappily isolated from the continuum of life.[6]

8. The healthy personality development of generativity depends upon the culture's values and upon the economic arrangements of the society.

a. In order that most people develop fully the role of parent, both mother and father must be respected in the society.

b. Giving must rank higher than getting, and loving higher than being loved.

c. The economy must be such that the future can be depended upon and each person can feel assured that he has a meaningful and respected part to play.

d. Only with cultural support can most individuals afford to renounce selfish aims and derive satisfaction from rearing children.

9. The most important responsibilities of this period grow out of the fact that middle-aged people are literally "in the middle"—not only of their own lives, but between generations. They act as a kind of bridge between the younger generation (which usually means their own children, if they have any) and the older generation—their own aging parents. In their middle years they become responsible to two generations, as well as to themselves.[6]

Isolation or Self-Absorption

1. Failure to develop the healthy personality component of generativity often results in a condition of stagnation or self-absorption.

2. Some young parents are retarded in their generative abilities, either because they never develop a sense of trust themselves or because they had to work too hard at building their own personalities. They indulge themselves as if they were their own children and may even lapse, from self-concern, into early physical or psychological invalidism.

3. The explanation may be found in the inadequate development of the personality components previously described. The failure goes far back. Because of unfortunate experiences in childhood, they did not arrive at a firm sense of trust, autonomy, initiative, or identity.

a. In others it may be only inadequacies in later stages, especially in the development of the sense of intimacy.

b. When a true sense of intimacy has not developed, the individual may obsessively seek companionship in a kind of self-absorption.

c. The individual is inclined to treat himself as a child and to be rivalrous with children if he/she has any.

d. He/she indulges self, expects to be indulged, and in general behaves in an infantile or immature manner.

The Virtue: Care

1. The virtue Erikson proposes to accompany the notion of generativity versus self-absorption in adulthood is the capacity to care.

2. To some, care means an anxious kind of solicitude; to Erikson care incorporates a more positive connotation.

3. Care is used in a sense which includes:

    a. the capacity *to care to do* something.

    b. the capacity to *care for* somebody or something.

    c. the capacity to *take care of* that which needs protection and attention.

    d. the thoughtfulness that assures one would *take care not to* do something destructive.[21]

4. Each adult accepts or rejects the challenge of accepting and caring for the next generation as his responsibility.

5. Adult man needs to be needed; for the strength of his ego and for that of his community, he requires the challenge emanating from what he has generated and from what now must be brought up, guarded, preserved, and eventually transcended.[24]

A Sense of Ego-Integrity in the Aged

Ego-Integrity Versus Despair
Virtue: Wisdom

Integrity is the culmination of the successful resolution of the seven previous crises in development throughout life. It implies an acceptance of the life one has lived with no regret for what could have been or what one should have done differently. It includes a new and different love of one's parents, free of the way that they should have been different and the acceptance of the fact that one's life is one's own responsibility.[11] It implies an acceptance of one's approaching death as the inevitable, and acceptance of a life lived as well as the individual knew how.[24] Those who can look back and feel satisfied that their lives have had meaning will have a sense of integrity. Those who see nothing but a succession of wrong turns and missed opportunities will feel despair.

The Sense of Integrity, "I Am What I Am"

1. The individual, in Erikson's words, "becomes able to accept his individual life cycle and the people who have become meaningfully significant to it."[9]

2. Although aware of the relativity of all the various life styles that have given meaning to human striving, the possessor of integrity is ready to defend the dignity of his own life-style against all physical and economic threats.[23]

3. Even in adulthood a reasonably healthy personality is sometimes secured in spite of previous misfortunes in the developmental sequence. New sources of trust may be found; fortunate events and circumstances may aid the individual in the struggle to feel autonomous. Imagination and initiative can be spurred by new responsibilities. Feelings of inferiority may be overcome by successful achievements. Even late in life, through self understanding, an individual may arrive at a true sense of who he is and what he has to do. He may be able to work through to a feeling of intimacy with others and care for the next generation in the form of grandchildren.[30]

The Culture and a Sense of Integrity

1. For the healthy personality development of children in any culture, it is necessary that a large proportion of adults attain a sense of integrity to a considerable degree. Not only parents but all who deal with children have need of this quality if they are to help children maintain the feeling that the universe is dependable and trustworthy.

2. Integrity is relatively easily attained and sustained when the culture itself gives support, when meaning to life is clearly spelled out in tradition and ceremony, and roles are clearly defined.

3. Our culture, with its rapidly changing technology, its separation of families and its diversity of standards, leaves much for the older individual to work out for themselves.

A Sense of Despair

1. The adult who lacks integrity in this sense may wish that he/she could live life again.

2. They feel that if at one time they had made different decisions they could have been different people and their ventures would have been successful.

3. They fear death and cannot accept the life cycle as the ultimate of life.

4. The "rest home" in our society and loss of health too often expose the aged person to extreme disgust and despair.

5. Despair plays on the feeling that time is too short to try out new roads to integrity.

6. Disgust is a means of hiding the despair, a chronic contemptuous displeasure with the way life is run.

7. Observation of aged people reveals the desire and the conscious effort to hold on to integrity and the frightening fight against slipping into the polarity of disgust and despair.

The Virtue: Wisdom

1. In the final stage of old age and maturity, ego-integrity versus despair is counterposed with wisdom. In old age, some wisdom prevails if only in the sense that the old person comes to appreciate and to represent something of the "wisdom of the ages."

2. Erikson: I'm not satisfied with the term wisdom because to some it seems to mean too difficult an achievement for each old person.[21]

3. Erikson says it is obvious that if a man lives long enough, he faces a renewal of infantile tendencies—a certain childlike quality if he is lucky, and senile childishness if he is not.

4. This final phase involves a sense of wisdom and a philosophy of life which often extends beyond the life-cycle of the individual and is directly related to the future of new developmental cycles.

5. Some of the wisdom of the aged has been eloquently expressed by an 85-year-old woman living in Lousiville, Kentucky[3]

> If I had my life to live over, I'd dare to make more mistakes next time. I'd relax. I'd limber up. I'd be sillier than I've been this trip. I'd take fewer things seriously. I'd take more chances. I'd take more trips. I'd climb more mountains and swim more rivers. I'd eat more ice cream and less beans. I'd perhaps have more actual troubles, but I'd have fewer imaginary ones.

> You see, I'm one of those people who live sensibly and sanely hour after hour, day after day. Oh, I've had moments, and if I had it to do over again, I'd have more of them. In fact, I'd try to have nothing else. Just moments, one after another, instead of living so many years ahead of each day. I've been one of those persons who never goes anywhere without a thermometer, a hot water bottle, a

35

raincoat, and a parachute. If I had it to do again, I would travel lighter than I have.

If I had my life to live over, I would start barefoot earlier in the spring and stay that way later in the fall. I would go to more dances, I would ride more merry-go-rounds, I would pick more daisies.

Bibliography

1. Ambron, Sueann Robinson. *Child Development.* New York: Holt, Rinehart and Winston, 1978, p. 321.
2. Auden, H. W. "Greatness Finding Itself," reprinted in *Forewards and Afterwards.* London: Faber and Faber, 1973, p. 79, 86.
3. Burnside, I. M. "The Later Decade of Life: Research and Reflections," in *Psychosocial Caring Through the Life Span.* I. M. Burnside, P. Ebersele, and H. E. Nance (ed.), New York: McGraw Hill, 1979, p. 245.
4. Conger, John Janeway. *Adolescence and Youth, Psychological Development in a Changing World.* New York: Harper and Row, 1977, p. 95, 96, 97.
5. Constantinople, A. "An Eriksonian Measure of Personality Development in College Students," *Developmental Psychology,* 1969, p. 359.
6. Craig, Grace, J. *Human Development.* Englewood Cliffs, New Jersey: Prentice Hall, Inc., 1976, p. 414, 447, 448, 449.
7. Elkind, David and Irving B. Wiener. *Development of the Child.* New York: John Wiley and Sons, Inc., 1978, p. 376, 378.
8. Elkind, David. "Erik Erikson's Eight Ages of Man," *Annual Editions, Readings in Human Development.* Guilford, Connecticut: The Duskin Publishing Group, 1976/77, p. 23, 24, 31.
9. Erikson, Erik H. *Childhood and Society.* New York: W. W. Norton & Co., 1963, p. 260–262.
10. Erikson, Erik H. *Dimensions of a New Identity.* New York: W. W. Norton & Co., 1974.
11. Erikson, Erik H. *Identity and the Life Cycle.* New York: International Universities Press, Inc., 1959, p. 66, 71, 75, 76, 95, 98.
12. Erikson, Erik H. *Identity and the Life Cycle.* New York: W. W. Norton & Co., 1980, p. 68, 76, 101.
13. Erikson, Erik H. *Identity Youth and Crisis.* New York: W. W. Norton & Co., 1968, p. 124, 125, 132.
14. Erikson, Erik H. *The Challenge of Youth.* New York: Anchor Books, Doubleday & Co., Inc., 1965, p. 3, 63, 67.
15. Erikson, Erik H. "The Golden Rule and the Cycle of Life," in *The Study of Lives.* New York: Atherton Press, 1963, p. 24.
16. Erikson, Erik H., M. J. E. Senn (ed.). *Symposium on the Healthy Personality.* New York: Josiah Macy Foundation, 1950.
17. Erikson, Erik H. *Sex Differences in the Play Configurations of Pre-Adolescents.* American Orthopsychiatry, 1951, p. 21. Also in R. E. Herron and Brian Sutton-Smith, *Child's Play.* New York: John Wiley, 1971, p. 126.
18. Erikson, Erik H. "The Problems of Ego-Identity," *Journal of American Psychoanalytic Association,* 4 (1), 1956, p. 56, 121.
19. Erikson, Erik H. *Youth: Fidelity and Diversity.* New York: Daedalus, 1962, p. 91.
20. Erikson, Erik H. and J. Erikson. "The Power of the Newborn," *Mademoiselle Magazine,* June, 1953, p. 100–102.
21. Evans, Richard I. *Dialogue With Erik Erikson.* New York: E. P. Dutton & Co., 1967, p. 15–53.
22. French, T. *The Integration of Behavior.* Chicago: University of Chicago Press, 1952, p. 66.
23. Harrison, Saul, I. McDermott (ed.). *Childhood Psychopathology, An Anthology of Basic Readings.* New York: International Universities Press, Inc., p. 113, 115, 116, 118, 123, 125, 126.
24. Huxley, Julian. *The Humanist Frame.* New York: Harper & Brothers, 1961, p. 155, 157, 158, 160.
25. Kastenbaum, Robert. *Human Developing, A Lifespan Perspective.* Boston, Massachusetts: Allyn and Bacon, 1979, p. 453, 456.

26. Maier, Henry W. *Three Theories of Child Development*. New York: Harper & Row Publishers, 1979, p. 91, 99, 100, 104, 110, 113, 120.
27. Muss, Rolf E. *Theories of Adolescents*. New York: Random House, 1975, p. 63, 67, 72, 73.
28. Newman, Barbara N. and Philip R. Newman. *Infancy & Childhood*. New York: John Wiley and Sons, Inc., 1978, p. 238.
29. Papalia, Diane R. and Sall Wendkos Olds. *Human Development*. New York: McGraw Hill Book Co., 1981, p. 480, 543.
30. Pukunas, Justun. *Human Development, An Emergent Science*. New York: McGraw Hill Book Co., 1976, p. 329.
31. Roazen, Paul. *Erik H. Erikson*. New York: The Free Press, A Division of Macmillan Publishing Co., 1976, p. vii, viii, ix, x.
32. Spitz, Ruth Eissler, et. al. *The Psychoanalytic Study of the Child*. New York: International Universities Press, 1945, p. 53–74.
33. Stone, Joseph L. and Joseph Church. *Childhood and Adolescence*. New York: Random House, 1979, p. 282, 341, 424.
34. White, R. W. *The Enterprise of Living: Growth and Organization of Personality*. New York: Holt, Rinehart and Winston, 1972.

II

ABRAHAM H. MASLOW
Theory of
Hierarchy of Basic Needs

ABRAHAM MASLOW

It is interesting to note that in researching Maslow's books, articles, speeches, and papers, very little is found in terms of his personal life. There is a scarcity of evidence of dates, education, family, honors, and degrees. This is probably as Maslow would have wanted it. Because of this, tribute to Maslow cannot be in terms of honors and accolades, but must be a tribute to his ideas, philosophies, assumptions, and concerns. Maslow is best known for his Motivational Theory of the Gratification of Basic Needs. His life was filled with humanitarian concerns. His dream was, that through understanding, all mankind would have a better opportunity to live in a society in which he or she was free to reach their highest potential.

This American was born on April 1, 1908, and died prematurely and unexpectedly on June 8, 1970. The psychological world was saddened by his untimely death for he had so much left to give in terms of helping mankind understand and appreciate their full potential.

Maslow's Concerns

Full Humanness for Mankind

According to Maslow, all evidence indicates that in practically every human being, and certainly in almost every new baby, there is an active will toward health, growth, and actualization of the human potential. He found it saddening to realize that only a small proportion of the human population arrives at the point of self-identity or of selfhood, full humanness, or self-actualization. He spent the last portion of his life trying to answer the question, "if we have the impulse toward full development of humanness, then why is it that so few people make it? What blocks healthy development?"[3]

He was committed to the idea that we need to have a sensitized appreciation for the greatest possibility of humanness and, simultaneously, a deep disappointment that these possibilities are so infrequently actualized. Maslow felt all falling away from full humanness, from the full blooming of human nature is a loss of human possibility, of what could have been, and of what should have been. Human and personal possibilities are lost. The world is narrowed and so is consciousness. Capacities are inhibited.[3]

The Good Person

Maslow saw the first and far-reaching problem is to make the Good Person. He felt people must be better human beings or else it was quite possible that society may be obliterated, and if not obliterated, certainly destined to live in tension and anxiety as a species. To Maslow, the Good Person could be called the self-evolving person, the responsible-for-self individual, the fully illuminated or awakened, perspicuous man, the fully human person, the self-actualizing person. He believed that no social reform, no beautiful constitution, program, or law is of consequence unless people are healthy enough, evolved enough, strong enough, good enough to understand them and to put legislation into practice in the right way.[3]

The Good Society

Maslow saw an urgent need for a Good Society. Good human beings need a good society in which to grow. "That society is good which fosters the fullest development of human potential and the fullest degree of humanness."[3] He felt goodness or badness depends upon the social institutions and arrangements in which people find themselves. For Maslow, the Good Society meant ultimately one species, one world. He believed that unless society put technological and biological improvements in the hands of good people, then improvements are either useless or dangerous. He felt that evil societies are more dangerous and more threatening today than ever before in human history simply because of the powers bestowed by advanced technology.[3]

Maslow urged all scientists to put their talents into the service of making the Good Person and making the Good Society.[3] He wrote, "that's one reason I have such great faith in the future of the United States. I think we're the first culture in history—first large culture—that has built itself pretty firmly on the notion of a higher nature of man, and that if you give man the freedom to choose, that he'll choose wisely."[3]

Maslow's Approach to Psychological Problems

A Humanistic Philosophy

Maslow's humanistic concerns for the improvement of mankind took him from philosophy to psychology. His adventures in psychology led him in many directions, some of which transcended the field of conventional study. In the beginning he was a Watsonian psychologist. Behaviorism looked like a good program for humanism in the thirties, and it was only when Maslow felt the failure of that approach that he searched elsewhere. As a student he was exposed to the theories of Frued and Adler: his doctoral dissertation combined the theories of these men. But he was never a disciple or a great programmatic follower. True to his philosophy, he was his own man. As Maslow became interested in certain psychological problems, he found that they could not be answered or managed well by classical scientific structure of the time. He raised legitimate questions and found he had to invent another approach in order to respond. His approach grew to be a general humanistic (concerned with the development and well-being of people) philosophy of psychology.

Maslow presented his Motivation Theory in 1942 to a psychoanalytic society. The theory was an effort on his part to integrate into a single theoretical structure the partial truths he saw in Freud, Adler, Jung, Levy, Fromm, Horney and Golstein. He had learned from experience in therapy that each of these writers was correct at various times and for various reasons.[2]

The Good Specimen

According to Maslow, if you want to answer the question: "How tall can the human species grow?" then, obviously it is well to pick out the already tall and study them. He did this with two of his teachers he "could not be content simply to adore, but sought to understand." Being a scientist, he sought a general account of the excellence he had discovered in these two teachers. He began to collect other such subjects for study and went on identifying and studying the good specimen, the "tallest" and the best people, for the rest of his life. He pointed out that this sort of research gave a fresh and encouraging view of mankind. "It showed what can be."[4] He studied psychologically whole people to find what made them whole.[3]

The Study of Self-Actualizing People

Maslow found that the available psychological language would not serve the direction of his research, and he determined to improve it. As he rasied legitimate questions, he began inventing another approach to psychological problems in order to deal with them. The key terms of the language he developed are "self-actualization," "peak-experience," and "the hierarchy of needs," ranging from "deficiency-need" to "being needs." He wanted to be able to say, "this is how people who are self-actualizing act and react to a wide gamut of situations, difficulties, and confrontations," and to demonstrate the psychological and educational importance of such research.

Freud's theory gave to the world the study of the sick and neurotic; from Maslow's work grew a psychology ordered by the symetrics of fully human health, intelligence, and aspiration. In Maslow's view, most if not all the evil in human life is due to ignorance. His base of explanation developed from the "givens" of self-actualization and the peak experience. His theory of motivation deals with the highest capacities of the healthy and strong as well as with defensive maneuvers of crippled spirits.[3]

A Different Psychological Approach

Maslow chose to speculate freely, to theorize, to play hunches and intuitions. He had a deliberate preoccupation with pioneering and originating rather than applying, validating, or verifying. He felt even though the validating, checking, and verifying are the backbone of science, it was a great mistake for scientists to consider themselves merely or mostly verifiers. Maslow realized that the pioneer, the creator, the explorer was often a single, often lonely person, and that he had to be a courageous person, not afraid to risk disapproval or make mistakes. He had to be a gambler who comes to tentative conclusions in the absence of facts and then spends years trying to find out if his hunches were correct.

He was convinced that the value-free, value-neutral, value-avoiding model of science from physics, chemistry, and astronomy (where it was necessary to keep the data exact while keeping the church out of scientific affairs) was quite unsuited for the scientific study of life.[3]

The Philosophy of Maslow

Maslow believed:
1. human life would never be understood unless its highest aspirations are taken into account.
2. the study of human life had to be both humanistic and holistic, an approach concerned with the well-being of people and an approach that viewed man as a totally integrated, organized whole, not a collection of separate organs and functions or separate from interaction with society.
3. the instinctoid nature of basic needs constitutes a system of intrinsic human values; it is human good that validates itself. Human values that are intrinsically good and desirable need no further justification. This is a hierarchy of values which is to be found in the very essence of human nature itself. These are not only wanted and desired by all human beings, but also needed in the sense that they are necessary to avoid illness and psychopathology.[2]
4. it is legitimate and fruitful to regard instinctoid basic needs as rights as well as needs. Human beings have a right to be human. In order to be fully human, these need gratifications are necessary and may be considered to be natural rights.[2]
5. personality problems may be loud protests against the crushing of psychological bones of one's inner nature.[4]
6. the historian of ideas would find many examples from different cultures and different times of a general trend to downlevel human motivation or uplevel human motivation.
7. self-actualizing people, even though all their basic needs have already been gratified, find life to be even more richly meaningful because they can live, so to speak, in the realm of "being," (full-humanness, fully functioning).

8. there are certain conditions that are prerequisites for basic need satisfactions. Such conditions as freedom to speak, freedom to do what one wishes so long as no harm is done to others, freedom to express oneself, freedom to investigate and seek for information, freedom to defend oneself, along with such abstractions as justice, fairness, honesty, orderliness, are examples of preconditions for basic need satisfaction.[2]

BASIC ASSUMPTIONS OF THE NEED THEORY

1. Each of us has an essential biologically based inner nature which is natural, intrinsic, and in a certain limited sense, unchangeable, or at least, unchanging relative to our basic selves.[4]

2. Each person's inner nature is in part unique to self and in part, unique to the species.

3. It is possible to study this inner nature scientifically and to discover what it is like.

4. This inner nature, as much as is known of it, seems not to be intrinsically or primarily or necessarily evil. The basic needs for life, for safety and security, for belongingness and affection, for respect and self-respect, and for self-actualization are basic human needs, and are neutral, or positively "good."

5. Since this inner nature is good or neutral rather than bad, it is best to bring it out and encourage it rather than suppress it. If it is permitted to guide our life, the growth is healthy, fruitful, and happy.

6. If this essential core of the person is denied or suppressed, the individual gets sick, sometimes in obvious ways, sometimes in subtle ways, sometimes immediately, sometimes later.

7. This inner nature is not strong and overpowering and unmistakable like the instincts of animals. It is weak and delicate and subtle and easily overcome by habit, cultural pressure, and wrong attitudes about it.[4]

8. Even though weak, it rarely disappears in the normal person—perhaps not even in the sick person. Even though denied, it persists underground, forever pressing for actualization.

9. Somehow the striving for actualization must all be incorporated with the necessity for discipline, deprivation, frustration, pain, and tragedy. To the extent that these experiences reveal and foster and fulfill our inner nature, they are desirable.

   a. The person who hasn't coped, struggled, and conquered continues to doubt that he could. This is true not only for external dangers; it applies to the ability to control and to delay impulses, and therefore, not to be afraid of them.

   b. If grief and pain are sometimes necessary for growth of the person, protection may be harmful. Pain is not necessarily bad. It may be desirable for strength. Not allowing people to go through pain may result in overprotection which implies a certain lack of respect for the integrity and future development of the individual.

10. The more we learn about man's natural tendencies, the easier it will be to understand how to

be good, how to be happy, how to be fruitful, how to respect ourselves, how to love, and how to fulfill our highest potential.[4]

11. The serious thing for each person to recognize vividly and poignantly is that every falling away from the species-virtue, every crime against one's own nature, every evil act, every one without exception, records itself in our unconscious and makes us despise ourselves.[4]

MASLOW'S HIERARCHY OF BASIC NEEDS
A THEORY OF HUMAN MOTIVATION

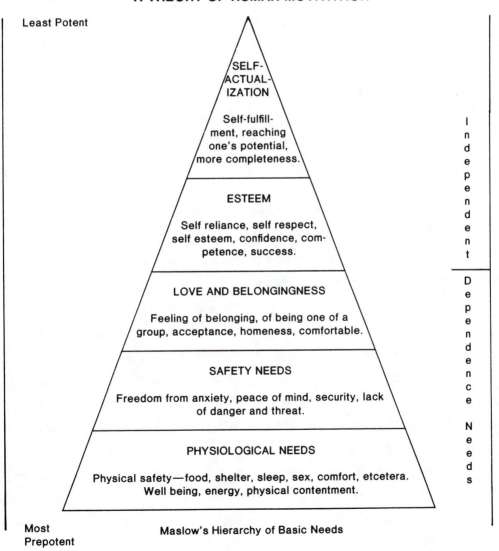

Least Potent

SELF-ACTUAL-IZATION

Self-fulfill-ment, reaching one's potential, more completeness.

ESTEEM

Self reliance, self respect, self esteem, confidence, competence, success.

LOVE AND BELONGINGNESS

Feeling of belonging, of being one of a group, acceptance, homeness, comfortable.

SAFETY NEEDS

Freedom from anxiety, peace of mind, security, lack of danger and threat.

PHYSIOLOGICAL NEEDS

Physical safety—food, shelter, sleep, sex, comfort, etcetera. Well being, energy, physical contentment.

Independent

Dependence Needs

Most Prepotent

Maslow's Hierarchy of Basic Needs

45

All mankind has basic needs which are arranged in a hierarchy from most prepotent to least potent.

The Basic Needs are these: Physiological Needs, Safety Needs, Belongingness and Love Needs, Esteem Needs, and the Need for Self-Actualization.

To the degree that these needs are gratified, man becomes psychologically healthy. To the degree that they are deprived, man becomes psychologically ill.

Motivation

1. Man is a dynamic energy system, and to the degree that energy must go toward filling lower more prepotent (powerful, coming before others) needs, energy cannot be directed toward filling less potent (powerful) or higher needs.
   a. The physiological needs, when unsatisfied, dominate the organism pressing all capacities and energy into their service.
   b. Gratification submerges and allows the next set of needs in the hierarchy to emerge and dominate. The individual now becomes safety obsessed.
   c. The principle is the same for the other sets of need in the hierarchy, i.e., love, esteem, and self-actualization.
   d. When man uses all energy seeking physical gratification, freedom from anxiety and acceptance of others, he functions at a deficiency level.
   e. To the degree that lower needs are filled, man is free to use his energy to give and receive love, move toward being competent and successful as a human, and reach for his potential. The individual is said then to be growth motivated rather than deficiency motivated.
   f. As needs are gratified, they cease to be active determinants of behavior.
2. Healthy people have had their basic needs sufficiently gratified so that they may experience safety, belongingness, love, respect, and self esteem and become intrinsically motivated.
3. According to Maslow, people function best when striving for something lacking, when wishing for something not possessed, and when organizing powers toward the gratification of that wish.
4. Need gratification leads to only temporary happiness which in turn tends to be succeeded by another higher discontent.
5. Gratification breeds increased rather than decreased motivation, heightened rather than lessened excitement.[2]

46

Dependence on the Environment

1. The need for safety, belongingness, love relations, and for respect can be satisfied initially by other people, i.e. only from outside the person.
2. This means considerable dependence on the environment.
3. The self-actualizing individual, being gratified in his basic needs is far less dependent, far less beholden, far more autonomous and self-directed and is free to move toward his potential.

Degree of Fixity

1. Maslow's hierarchy of needs appear to be in a fixed order, but actually it is not that rigid. It is true that most people appear to have these basic needs in the order of the hierarchy; however, there have been exceptions.
   a. There are some people for whom self-esteem seems to be more important than love. But essentially they seek high self-esteem, and their behavior expressions are evidence of their need to be loved.
   b. In some people the less prepotent goals may simply be lost and may disappear forever. The person whose life force is spent in striving for lower needs, e.g., chronic unemployment, may continue to be satisfied for the rest of one's life.
   c. The so-called psychopath personality is another example of permanent loss of love needs. These are those who have been starved for love in the earliest months of their lives and have simply lost forever the desire and the ability to give and receive affection.
   d. When a person has been satisfied for a long time, this need may be under-evaluated. People who have never experienced chronic hunger are apt to underestimate its effect.
   e. When a person has not satisfied a need, he may move to a higher level in a negative way (e.g. the criminal who delights in seeing his name in headlines and his picture on the front page of the newspaper).
2. People who have been reasonably well satisfied in their basic needs throughout their lives, particularly in their earliest years, seem to develop exceptional power to withstand pressure of future thwarting of these needs.
3. Maslow gives the impression that if one need is satisfied, then another emerges. This is not always the case. Most members of our society are partially satisfied in all their basic needs

47

at once. A more realistic description of the hierarchy is seen in terms of decreasing percentages of satisfaction.

4. The needs are neither conscious nor unconscious, but more often unconscious, especially moving up the hierarchy.[2]

Cultural Specificity

1. It is the common experience of anthropologists that people from different cultures are more alike than unalike.

2. The most startling differences are superficial rather than basic, e.g. differences in style of hairdress, clothes, food, etcetera.

3. There appears to be a unity of needs and wants behind the apparent diversity of means from culture to culture.[2]

Maslow's Five Basic Needs in Detail

The Physiological Needs

1. These are the most prepotent of all needs. They include food, water, shelter, sex, sleep, and so on. They could reach any number, depending on the degree of specificity. The fulfillment of the physical needs gives one the feeling of well-being: health, energy, euphoria, and physical contentment. Physical needs could also be thought of as survival needs.

2. The human being who is missing everything in life in the extreme is most likely to have physiological needs as a major motivation rather than others. A person who is lacking food, safety, love, and esteem would most probably hunger for food more strongly than for anything else. Likewise, a starving person is not overly concerned with having status.

3. If all the needs are unsatisfied, and the organism is then dominated by the physiological needs, all other needs may become simply nonexistent or pushed into the background.

   a. The whole organism is characterized by saying that it is hungry; consciousness is almost completely preempted by hunger.

   b. All capacities are put into the service of hunger-satisfaction.

   c. The receptors and effectors: the intelligence, memory, habits, may now be defined simply as hunger-gratifying tools.

d. Capacities that are not useful for this purpose lie dormant or are pushed into the background. For the man who is extremely and dangerously hungry, no other interest exists but food.

4. Another peculiar characteristic of the human organism when it is dominated by a certain need is that the whole philosophy of the future tends to change.

   a. For the chronically and extremely hungry man, Utopia can be defined simply as a place where there is plenty of food.

   b. He tends to think that if he is guaranteed food for the rest of his life, he will be perfectly happy and will never want anything more.

   c. Anything other than food is likely to be defined as unimportant. Freedom, love, respect, may be waved aside since they fail to fill the stomach.

   d. It is quite true that man lives by bread alone when there is nothing besides bread.

5. Culture itself is an adaptive tool; one whose main function is to make the physiological emergencies come less often.

6. What happens to a man's desires when there is plenty of bread and when his belly and other physiological needs are continually filled?

   a. At once other (and higher) needs emerge and these, rather than physiological hungers, dominate the organism.

   b. And when these in turn are satisfied, again new (and still higher) needs emerge, and so on.

   c. This is what Maslow means by saying that the basic human needs are organized into a hierarchy of relative prepotency.

7. Gratification becomes as important a concept as deprivation in motivation theory.

   a. Gratification of the needs on level one and two releases the organism from the domination of physiological needs, thereby permitting the emergence of other more social goals.

   b. The physiological needs now exist only potentially in the sense that they may emerge again to dominate the organism if they are thwarted.

   c. A want that is satisfied is no longer a want.

   d. The organism is dominated and organized only by unsatisfied needs.[2]

The Safety Needs

1. If the physiological needs are relatively well gratified, there emerges a new set of needs which may be categorized roughly as the safety needs (security, stability, dependency, protection, freedom from fear, anxiety, and chaos, need for structure, order, law, limits, strength in the protector, and so on).

2. All that has been said of the physiological needs is equally true for the safety needs.

3. The organism may well be equally dominated by them.

4. They may serve as almost exclusive organizers of behavior, recruiting all the capacities of the organism in their service.

5. The whole organism may be described as a safety-seeking mechanism.

   a. The receptors and the effectors of the intellect are primarily safety-seeking tools.

   b. As in the hungry individual, the dominating goal is a strong determinant not only of the person's current world view but also of his value judgement of the future.

   c. Most things look less important than safety and protection—including the physiological needs, which being satisfied, are now underestimated.

   d. An individual in this state, if it is extreme enough and chronic enough, may be characterized as living almost for safety alone.

6. An understanding of the safety needs can be made more efficiently perhaps though observation of infants and children, in whom the needs are much more simple and obvious. The child who feels fear clings to some source of comfort—an adult, a blanket, or a favorite toy.

   a. Infants and children do not inhibit this reaction at all; infants will react in a total fashion if feeling endangered.

   b. Adults in our society have been taught inhibitions for social sanctions; even when adults feel their safety is threatened, it is not always possible to observe the need in overt behavior.

7. An indication of a child's need for safety is his preference for some kind of undisrupted routine or rhythm.

   a. The child wants a predictable, lawful, orderly world.

   b. Injustice, unfairness, or inconsistency on the part of parents seems to make a child feel anxious and unsafe.

c. Young children seem to thrive better under a system that has an outline of structure in which there is a schedule of a kind. Some sort of routine, something that can be counted on, will give children feelings of safety not only for the present but for the future.

8. Parents and family systems must be responsible for safety needs.

   a. Only the child who feels safe takes the healthy risk to go forward.

   b. Quarreling, physical assult, separation, divorce, or death within the family may be particularly terrifying to all members of a family, both adults and children.

   c. Parental outbursts of rage or threats of punishment directed to the child, name calling, harsh words, rough handling, or severe physical punishment often elicit such total panic and terror that it is likely more is involved than the physical pain alone.

   d. To some children this terror represents a fear of loss of parental love.

   e. It occurs in a rejected child who seems to cling to the hateful parents for safety and protection of a kind rather than because of the hope of love. The child chooses negative love over the possibility of no love.

9. Confronting the average child with unfamiliar or unmanageable stimuli will too frequently elicit the danger or terror reaction. For example, getting lost or being separated from the parents for a short time can cause a child to panic. The child's frantic clinging to the parent is testimony to the role of protector—quite apart from the role of food giver and love giver.

10. The peaceful, stable society which at one time made its members feel safe is being threatened today from within and without.

    a. In a very real sense society is no longer safe.

    b. Only to the degree that safety needs are satisfied can a society devote energy to higher level capabilities.

    c. Social chaos, economic instability, duplicity in government, bring about a neurotic, unhealthy society.

11. The expressions of social safety are seen in the common preference for a job with tenure and the promise of longevity, the desire for a saving account, a pensioned retirement, and insurance of various kinds—medical, dental, unemployment, disability.

12. Other aspects of the attempt to seek safety and stability in the world are seen in the very common preference for familiar rather than unfamiliar things or for the known rather than the unkown.

13. Some neurotic adults in our society are like the unsafe child in this desire for safety, although in the former it may appear less obvious.

   a. Adult reaction to unknown and perhaps unreal dangers in a world that is perceived to be hostile, is often overwhelming and threatening.

   b. Such a person behaves as if a great catastrophe were almost always impending.

   c. This individual's safety needs often find specific expression in a search for a protector or a stronger person on whom he may depend.

   d. The neurotic individual may be described as a grown-up person who retains his childhood attitudes toward the world.

      (1) He behaves as if he were actually afraid of a spanking or of being abandoned by his parents, or having his food taken away from him.

      (2) It is as if his childish attitudes of fear of a dangerous world had gone underground and were untouched by the growing and learning processes. They are now ready to be called out by any stimulus that would make a child feel endangered and threatened.

14. The neurosis in which the search for safety takes its clearest form is the compulsive-obsessive neurosis.

   a. Compulsive-obsessive individuals try frantically to order and stabilize the world so that no unmanageable, unexpected, or unfamiliar dangers will ever appear.

   b. They manage to maintain their equilibrium by avoiding everything unfamiliar and strange and by ordering their restricted world in such a neat, disciplined and orderly fashion that everything in the world can be counted on.

   c. They try to arrange the world so that the unexpected cannot possibly occur.

   d. If, through no fault of their own, something unexpected does occur, they go into a panic reaction as if this unexpected occurrence constituted a grave danger. To them it does constitute a grave danger to their security because they only feel safe in close, personally defined situations which they control.

   e. What is seen as a mild preference in the healthy person, e.g. preference for the familiar, becomes a life and death necessity in abnormal cases.

   f. The healthy taste for the novel and unknown is missing or at a minimum in the neurotic.

g. Some individuals will use all energy and capacities to survive and function at this level, never tasting the honey of life that comes with the freedom and excitement of higher levels.

15. Assured safety permits higher needs and impulses to emerge in the individual and in turn directs growth toward mastery of self and environment. To endanger safety means regression to the more basic foundation. This means that if the choice between giving up safety or giving up growth must be made, safety will ordinarily win out. Safety needs are prepotent over growth needs.[4]

Belongingness and Love Needs

1. If both the physiological and the safety needs are fairly well gratified, the love and affection and belongingness needs emerge. The whole cycle already described will repeat itself with this new center.

   a. As never before, the person will feel keenly the absence of friends, a sweetheart, or a wife or child.

   b. The individual will hunger for affectionate relations with people, namely for a place in a group or family; the individual will strive with great intensity to achieve this goal.

   c. To attain such a goal becomes more important than anything else in the world and the individual may forget that when he was hungry he sneered at love as unreal, unnecessary, or unimportant.

2. There is very little scientific information about the belongingness need.

   a. It is a common theme in novels, autobiographies, poems, and plays.

   b. From a knowledge of belonging needs, we know of the destructive effects on children of such things as moving too often and consequent disorientation, of the general over-mobility that is forced by industrialization, of rootlessness, or of despising one's roots, one's origins, one's group, or of being torn from one's home and family, or being a newcomer rather than a native.

   c. It is easy to underplay the deep importance of the neighborhood, of one's territory, of one's own "kind," one's class, one's gang, one's familiar working colleagues. We have a deep animalistic tendency to herd, to flock, to join, to belong.

3. Today we find an increase in personal growth groups: intentional communities which may be motivated by the unsatisfied hunger for contact, for intimacy, for belongingness. The need to overcome the widespread feeling of alienation, strangeness, and lonliness might be worsened by mobility, by the breakdown of traditional groupings, the scattering of families, the generation gap, the steady urbanization and disappearance of village face-to-faceness, and the resulting shallowness of American friendship.

4. In our society the thwarting of the need to belong and to be loved is the most common found core in cases of maladjustment and pathology.

   a. Love and affection, as well as their possible expression in sexuality, are generally looked upon with ambivalence and are customarily surrounded with restrictions, uncertainties, and inhabitions.

   b. Practically all theorists of psychopathology stress the thwarting of the love need as basic in the picture of maladjustment.

   c. It is saddening to look at the number of deviants in our society today who were not loved, cannot love, and consequently become unlovable.

5. Psychological health comes from being loved rather than from being deprived of love.

6. Being loved promotes a feeling of secure fun, merriment, elation, a feeling of well-being, and gaiety. Being loved also can promote the security of expressing anger and risking another's displeasure.

7. There are love relationships between friends, brothers, parents and children. One of the purer loves is the relationship between grandparents and grandchildren where the joy for joy's sake is paramount.

8. Healthy love permits the greatest spontaneity, the greatest naturalness. In such a relationship it is not necessary to be guarded, to conceal, to try to impress, to feel tense, to watch one's words, to suppress or repress. Just the opposite is true; the real self is open for exchange.

   a. Love permits a person to unfold, to open up, to drop defenses. One can be oneself without feeling there are demands or expectations. One may be naked not only physically but psychologically and spiritually and still feel loved, wanted, and secure.

   b. One can be deeply understood and deeply accepted.

9. Love consists primarily of a feeling of tenderness and affection with great enjoyment, happiness, satisfaction, elation, and even ecstasy in experiencing this feeling. Pleasant experience is more pleasant because of the presence of the sweetheart, a friend, a spouse, or one's child.

10. Love knowledge produces greater accuracy of perception. Some kinds of knowledge are available that are not available to nonlovers. Love, whether for a sweetheart or a child, produces interest and fascination.

11. The love of a person implies not the possession of that person but the affirmation of that person. It means granting him gladly the full right to his uniqueness.

12. The consequent reaction is to enjoy, to be enjoyable, to admire, to be admirable, to be delighted, to contemplate, and to appreciate rather than to use.

13. Love is not synonymous with sex. Sex may be studied as a purely physiological need. Ordinarily healthy sexual behavior is multi-determined; that is to say, behavior is determined not only by sexual needs but also other needs such as love, affection, and esteem.

14. Love needs involve both giving and receiving.

The Esteem Needs

1. All people in society (with a few pathological exceptions) need a stable, firmly based, high evaluation for self-respect, self-esteem and for the esteem of others.

2. These needs may be classified into two subsidary sets:

   a. *Self Esteem.* This is the desire for strength, for mastery and competence, for confidence in the face of the world, and for independence leading to freedom.

   b. *Esteem from Others.* We have what we may call the desire for reputation or prestige (defined as respect or esteem from other people), status, fame and glory, dominance, recognition, attention, importance, dignity, or appreciation.

3. Satisfaction of self-esteem needs leads to feelings of self-confidence, worth, strength, capability and adequacy, of being useful and necessary in the world.

4. Thwarting of these needs produces feelings of inferiority, of weakness, and of helplessness. These feelings in turn give rise to either basic discouragement or else compensatory or neurotic trends.

5. From the theologian's discussion of pride, from the Frommian theories about self-deception to one's own nature, from the Rogerian work with self, from essayists like Ayn Rand, we learn

more and more of the dangers of basing self-esteem on the opinions of others rather than on opinions of self, based on competency. Competence is determined by what the individual knows to be true about self rather than on external fame or unwarranted adulation.

6. The actual competence and achievement that is based on sheer willpower, determination, and responsibility is the meaningful self-esteem that comes naturally and easily out of one's own inner nature, out of one's real self rather than out of the idealized pseudo-self.[2]

The Need for Self-Actualization

1. Self-Actualizers can be defined as people who are no longer motivated by the need for safety, belongingness, love, status, and self-respect because these needs have been satisfied. Self-actualizers have no serious deficiencies to make up. They are free to move toward their highest potential. A new restlessness develops.

   a. Actualization of a person's real potentialities is conditioned by the presence of basic-need satisfying parents and significant others, all those factors called "ecological," on the "health" of the culture or lack of it, and on the world situation. Growth toward self-actualization and full humanness is made possible by a complex hierarchy of "good pre-conditions."[4]

   b. These physical, chemical, biological, interpersonal, cultural conditions matter for the individual finally to the extent that they do or do not supply him with the basic necessities and rights. These permit him to become strong enough to take over his own fate.[4]

   c. Self-actualization can be thought of as an episode or a spurt in which the powers of the person come together in a particularly efficient and intensely enjoyable way, in which one is more integrated and more whole, more open for experience, more perfectly expressive or spontaneous, more creative, more humorous, more ego-transcending, more independent of his lower needs. He becomes in these episodes more truly himself, more completely actualizing in his potentialities, closer to the core of his being, more fully human.[3]

   d. Self-actualization is a matter of degree and of frequency rather than an all-or-none affair. Self-actualizing subjects transcend nationalism, class, and culture. They are flexible and can adapt themselves realistically to any people or environment. They are capable of gratitude. Life remains precious and never grows stale.[2]

2. In Maslow's last book, *The Farther Reaches of Human Nature,* published after he died, he describes in greater detail "what one does when one self-actualizes."[3]

   a. Self-actualization means experiencing existence fully, vividly, selflessly, and with full concentration and total absorption. It is "losing oneself to find oneself." One becomes totally absorbed in something and forgets the poses and defenses. The key word is "selflessly." People generally suffer from too little selflessness and too much self-consciousness and self-awareness.

   b. Life is a process of choice, one after another. At each point there is a progression choice and a regression choice. There may be a movement toward defense, toward safety, toward being afraid. On the other side, there is a growth choice. To make the growth choice instead of the fear choice a dozen times a day is to move a dozen times a day toward self-actualization.

   c. To talk of self-actualization implies that there is a self to be actualized. A human being is not a lump of clay. He is something which is already there, a structure of some kind. There is an inner self, and one must react to the life-force within as a means to letting the self imerge. Most people (and especially young children) listen not to themselves but to others.

     (1) Finding out whom one is, what he is, what he likes, what he doesn't like, what is good for him, and what is bad, where he is going and what his mission is means the exposure of self. It means identifying defenses, and after defenses have been identified, it means gathering the courage to give them up.

     (2) It means exposing self-illusion, getting rid of a false notion, in fact, discovering what one is.

   d. When in doubt, a self-actualizing person is honest rather than dishonest. Looking within oneself for many of the answers implies taking responsibility. Each time one takes responsibility, self-actualization occurs.

   e. One cannot choose wisely for life unless one dares to say calmly, "yes or no. I choose or reject." Making an honest statement may involve daring to be different, unpopular, or nonconforming. To be courageous rather than afraid is another version of the same thing.

   f. Self-actualization is not only an end state but also the process of actualizing one's potentialities at any time, in any amount. For example, it is a matter of becoming more knowledgeable through studious habits. Self-actualizing means using one's intelligence. It may mean going through an arduous and demanding period of preparation in order to realize one's potentialities. Self-actualization means working well to do the thing one wants to do.

g. Peak experiences are transient moments of self-actualization. They are moments of ecstasy which cannot be bought, cannot be guaranteed, cannot even be sought. One must be willing to be "surprised by the joy." Sometimes one does not realize that an experience was a peak experience until afterward, looking back. One can set up conditions so that peak experiences are more likely, or one can, perversely, set up the conditions so that they are less likely to occur.[3]

Summary

a. Self-actualization is not a matter of one great moment. Self-actualization is a matter of degree, of little gains accumulated one by one.

b. People who fit the criteria go about it in these ways:

(1) They trust their own instinct; they listen to their own voice.

(2) They take responsibility; they labor honestly.

(3) They make growth choices rather than safety or fear choices.

(4) They are involved in a cause outside their own skin, in something outside of themselves. They are devoted and selfless. They devote their lives to the search for the "being" values.

(5) They are true to their own inner nature and do not deny it out of weakness or for advantage or for any other reason. The person who belies his talent: the born painter who sells stockings instead of painting, the intelligent man who lives a stupid life, the man who sees truth and keeps his mouth shut, the coward who gives up his manliness, all these people perceive in a deep way that they have done wrong to themselves and despise themselves for it.[4]

(6) Self-actualization is based upon the unconscious and preconscious perception of one's own nature, of one's own destiny, of capacities, of one's "call" in life.

Deficiency Motivation and Growth Motivation

Maslow discussed the difference that he observed between the lives of healthy people, people motivated by growth, contrasted with people motivated by deficiency. He divided motivation into deficiency motivation and growth motivation.

Deficiency Motivation—Psychologically Neurotic People

1. Neurosis seems, in its beginning and at its core, to be a deficiency disease.
2. Neurosis is born out of being continually deprived of certain satisfactions called needs.
3. It is the result of, along with other complex determinants, ungrafitied wishes for life and safety, for belongingness and identification, for close, love relationships, and for respect and prestige.
4. Need deficiency characteristics are basic or instinctoid if:
   a. the need absense breeds illness.
   b. its presence prevents illness.
   c. its restoration cures illness.
   d. under certain free choice situations, the need is preferred by the deprived person over other satisfactions.
   e. it is found to be inactive, at a low ebb, or functionally absent in the healthy person.
   f. conscious or unconscious learning and desire appear.
   g. a sense of deficiency is apparent, as if something were missing.
5. The deficiencies are essentially deficits in the perception of the organism, empty holes which must be filled for health's sake. They must be filled from without by human beings other than the subject.[4]

Growth Motivation—Psychologically Healthy People

1. Healthy people have sufficiently gratified their basic needs for safety, belongingness, love, respect and self-esteem so that they are intrinsically motivated.
2. They are motivated to strive toward self-actualization as an unceasing trend toward unity and integration within the person.
3. In contrast to neurotic people, healthy people are defined by the following characteristics:
   a. superior perception of reality.

b. increased acceptance of self, of others, and of nature.

c. increased spontaneity.

d. increase in problem-centering.

e. increased detachment and desire for privacy.

f. increased autonomy and resistance to enculturation.

g. greater freshness and appreciation and richness of emotional reaction.

h. higher frequency of peak experiences.

i. increased identification with the human species.

j. changes or improved interpersonal relations.

k. more democratic character structure.

l. greatly increased creativeness.

m. certain changes in the value system.

4. Growth is the result of the various processes which bring the person toward ultimate self-actualization.

5. It is going on all the time in the life history of the healthy person.

6. It is not all or none, in which basic needs are completely gratified; it is one by one, a single recession before the next higher one emerges into consciousness.

7. Growth is a progressive gratification of basic needs to the point where the need ceases to be the prime force of motivation.[4]

Growth Motivation Versus Deficiency Motivation

The psychological life of the person is lived differently when a person is deficiency-need bent rather than when the person is growth-dominated. The following differences make this clear:

Attitude toward Impulse and Need

1. Deficiency motivated people:

a. associate negative attitudes with the need.

b. find desire or impulse to be a nuisance or even a threat and will try to get rid of it by denial or avoidance.

c. find it difficult to overcome the annoying and achieve a cessation of tension, an equilibrium, a homeostasis, a quiescence, a state of rest, a lack of pain.

d. press toward the elimination of that need or drive.

2. Growth motivated people:

a. find impulses are desired and welcomed, are enjoyable and pleasant; want more of them rather than fewer. If tensions are present, they are pleasurable tensions.

b. welcome creative impulses; the talented person enjoys using and expanding his talents.

c. perceive different basic needs as related to each other in an hierarchial order so that gratification of one need and its consequent fulfillment does not bring a state of rest or stoic apathy to the person. Rather, there is an emergence into consciousness of another "higher" need, a wanting and desiring continues within the organism.

d. become more active rather than coming to rest.

e. find growth is a rewarding and exciting process.

f. enjoy life in general and in practically all its aspects, while other people enjoy only stray moments of triumph, of achievement.[4]

Species-Wide Goals and Idiosyncratic Goals

1. The deficit-needs are shared by all members of the human species and to some extent by other species as well.

2. Self-actualization is idiosyncratic since every person is different.

3. The deficits, i.e. the species requirements, must ordinarily be fairly well satisfied before real individuality can develop fully.

4. Just as all trees need sun, water, and food from the environment, so do all people need safety, love, and status from their environment.

5. Once satiated with these elementary, species-wide necessities, each tree and each person proceeds to develop in his own style, uniquely using these necessities for his own private purpose.

6. In a very meaningful sense, development becomes more determined from within rather than from without.[4]

Dependence On and Indepedence of the Environment

Other-directed Versus Self-directed

1. The deficiency-motivated person:
   a. is considerably more dependent on other people for need satisfaction.
   b. does not govern himself or control his own fate.
   c. must be beholden to the sources of supply of needed gratification. Their wishes, their whims, their rules and laws govern him and must be appeased lest he jeopardize his source of supply.
   d. must be "other directed," and must be sensitive to other peoples approval, affection, and good will.
   e. must adapt and adjust by being flexible and responsive and by changing himself to fit the external situation.
   f. must be more afraid of the environment since there is always the possibility that it may fail or disappoint him.
   g. becomes anxious, even hostile because of this dependence.
2. The self-actualizing individual:
   a. is gratified in his basic need and is far less dependent, far less beholden, far more autonomous and self-directed.
   b. becomes more self-sufficient and self-contained.
   c. depends less on other people, is less ambivalent about them, less anxious and also less hostile, less needful of their praise and their affection, less anxious for honors, prestige, and rewards.
   d. finds the sources of their actions are more internal than reactive.[4]

Interested and Disinterested Interpersonal Relations

1. The deficiency-motivated person:
   a. is far more dependent upon other people than is the man who is predominantly growth-motivated.
   b. colors and limits interpersonal relations. To see people primarily as need-gratifiers or as

sources of supply is an abstract act. People are seen not as wholes, as complicated, unique individuals, but rather from the point of view of usefulness.

    c. finds boring, irritating, or threatening that which is not related to the perceivers needs.

2. The self-actualizing individual:

    a. can have fully disinterested, desireless, objective, and holistic perceptions of another human being. This becomes possible when he is not needed.

    b. bases approval, admiration and love less upon gratitude for usefulness and more on the objective, intrinsic qualities of the perceived person.

    c. is admired for objective qualities rather than because he flatters or praises. He is loved because he is love-worthy rather than because he seeks love[4]

Ego-Centering and Ego-Transcendence

1. The growth-oriented, self-actualized person:

    a. can be most problem-centered, most self-forgetful, most spontaneous in his activities.

    b. becomes absorbed in perceiving, in doing, in enjoying, and in creating.

    c. can leave self-consciousness behind as he deals with the objective world.

2. The need-deficient person finds it difficult to center upon the world, is self-conscious, egocentric, and gratification-oriented. This pattern becomes more marked the more need-deficits the person has.[4]

Perception

1. Deficiency-motivated people:

    a. perceive in a need-determined way.

    b. see others as simply money-givers, food-suppliers, safety-givers, someone to depend on, or an anonymous servant or means object.

        (1) Other people resent this; they want to be taken for themselves, as complete and whole individuals.

        (2) They dislike being perceived as useful objects or as tools.

2. Self-actualizing people:

    a. do not have need-gratifying qualities nor do they use other people for self-gratification.

    b. find it possible to take a non-valuing, non-judging, non-interferring, non-condemning attitude toward others.[4]

B-Love and D-Love

1. D-Love
   a. D-love is a deficiency-motivated love, a selfish, needed love.
   b. It is an emptiness into which love, praise, and support have to be poured to maintain it.
   c. The love-deprived person falls in love because he needs and craves love, because he lacks it, and he is impelled to make up this pathogenic deficiency.
   d. One cannot grow and give love freely because of the regressive power of ungratified deficiency-needs, of the attraction of safety and security, of the functions of defense and protection against pain, fear, and loss.
   e. D-love people are clinging and dependent, have hooks and anchors, and tend toward jealousy. They need to take love but find it difficult to give love to others. They need to be supported but find it difficult to support.
   f. In D-love, one must always expect some degree of anxiety-hostility.
   g. In D-love, a person is functioning on a safety level.

2. B-Love
   a. B-love is love for the being of another person, unneeding love, unselfish love.
   b. Healthy people have been love-need satisfied. They require less love while more able to give love. In this sense they are more loving people.
   c. B-love is welcomed into consciousness and is completely enjoyed. Since it is non-possessive and is admiring rather than needing, it is pleasurable to give.
   d. In the B-love relationship there is a fusion of the ability to love and respect others while respecting oneself. Two people can be extremely close together and yet be apart when necessary without jeopardizing the relationship. They do not need to cling to one another.
   e. In B-love individuality is strengthened; the ego is in a sense merged with another, yet in another sense remains separate and strong and whole.
   f. Self-actualizing men and women tend not to seek sex for its own sake but rather as a coupling with healthy, exchange-oriented love.
   g. B-love allows a person to be himself without feeling that there are unrealistic demands or expectations upon him.
   h. B-love is a richer, "higher," more valuable subjective experience than D-love.

i. B-lovers are eager to help the other toward self-actualization, proud of spousal triumphs, more altruistic, generous, and fostering.

j. B-love is as much a cognitive as an emotional-conative reaction. Far from accepting the common platitude that love makes people blind, it is non-love that makes people blind. Those people who can give a B-type of love are those who are realistically aware of self and others.

k. B-love, in a profound but testable sense, creates the individual. It reinforces a self-image, it reinforces self-acceptance, a feeling of love-worthiness, all of which permit growth. It is questionable whether the full development of the human being is possible without it.[4]

Bibliography

1. Frick, Willard B., Humanistic Psychology: interviews with Maslow, Murphy, and Rogers. Ohio: Charles E. Merrill, 1971.
2. Maslow, Abraham H. Motivation and Personality, (2nd ed.), New York: Harper and Row, 1970, p. xi, xiii, xiv, xix, xxi, 35–36, 46–47, 51–55.
3. Maslow, Abraham H. The Farther Reaches of Human Nature. New York: The Viking Press, Inc., 1971, p. 5, 6, 8, 19, 20, 21, 25, 26, 41–50.
4. Maslow, Abraham H. Toward A. Psychology of Being. New York: D. Van Nostrand Company, Inc., 1968, p. 3–4, 5, 7, 8, 27, 29–30, 36, 37, 39–40, 41–43, 45, 46, 49.

JEAN PIAGET
Theory of Cognitive Development

PIAGET

It was a warm September day in 1980. I was attending a conference on the family when I heard the sad news that Piaget had died. Later that day as I walked past the college's beautiful fountain with a large reflecting pool, I found myself comparing Piaget's life to that magnificent structure. For over 60 years his ideas had poured forth with tremendous force. He had given to the world an understanding of how individuals come to know what they know and how they use the known to adapt to their world. The analogy seemed appropriate, for then, as if by some strange circumstance, the fountain was turned off in preparation for a symphony that evening. Piaget's fountain of creative ideas had now also been turned off. But below the fountain of his ideas, a reflecting pool of insights, books, and research remained for study and reflection with time to incorporate and time to evaluate his contributions. There is little doubt that scholars will continue studying his work, finding errors, and making revisions as he would have encouraged them to do. Still, there is every indication that when the pool settles, Piaget will rank with other great men for his psychological contributions, his gift to mankind.

Piaget the Man

Piaget was a man who dedicated his life to the study of knowledge and how it developed. It has been estimated that he has written the equivalent of more than fifty 500 page books. He is considered one of the most influential psychologists today. His work is cited in every major textbook on psychology, education, linguistics, sociology, child development, and other disciplines as well.[5]

The impact of this man's thinking upon present day psychology and education is becoming increasingly evident.[6] Piaget's works have generated more interest and research than those of any other person in psychology in the last fifty years. His studies have radically changed our thinking about the growth of human intelligence.

David Elkind was a close associate of this remarkable man. In paraphrase, he shares this personal view:

Jean Piaget's personal life reflected the scope, ease, and contemplation required for his endeavors. He was a man with an aura that made one aware of his intellectual and physical presence. He was tall, wore bulky dark suits, had wavy white hair, and eyes that sparked behind horn-rimmed glasses. His defining accessories were his meerschaum pipe, a blue beret, and a bicycle.

He had a tremendous love, empathy, and appreciation of children, a compelling need for solitude and contact with nature. Even though he was internationally famous, he rejected the trappings of fame; he was most comfortable in a situation where scholars could exchange ideas. With a quiet humor, he identified with all mankind.

Jean Piaget's life was one of scholarship and hard work. Beginning with an intellectually precocious youth, he published articles on the sparrow in scientific journals at the age of ten, articles on mollusks at sixteen, received his doctorate from the University of Neuchatel in Switzerland by the time he was twenty-four years old. The year was 1918.

The Swiss psychologist engaged in several academic activities including a period in Binets (grade school) laboratory in Paris where he worked standardizing intelligence tests. He became fascinated in the process by which children derive incorrect answers, especially since the patterns of response suggested that age differences were involved. The observations suggested to Piaget that the study of children's thinking might provide some of the answers he sought on the philosophical plane. He planned to investigate them, then move on to other problems. Interestingly, the study of children became the lifelong preoccupation of this versatile individual.

After Paris he moved permanently to Geneva and later became director of the J. J. Rousseau Institute at the University of Geneva. Here he stayed until his retirement a few years before his death. The institute proved to be an ideal environment for his studies. The publication of his first studies of the mental development of children, *The Language and Thought of the Child,* and later, *Judgement and Reasoning in the Child,* and *The Child's Conception of the World,* gained worldwide recognition and made Piaget a world-renowned psychologist before he was thirty.

As Piaget's work grew in reputation, students came to work with him and collaborate on his research efforts. Piaget married one of these students, and they had three children called Jacqueline, Laurent, and Monique. The three became the subjects for his first research. They are now grown but have been immortalized by Piaget in his first three books that are now classics in child development literature.

Piaget had been recognized around the world and held honorary degrees from many leading universities. He traveled to the United States to share his knowledge with many groups interested in child development. But only in the last two decades has American psychology and education come to recognize that Piaget is in fact one of the giants of developmental psychology. Perhaps part of the reason for this delay was that his books were written in French, and Piaget did not speak or understand English well. Several fortunate Americans received grants and studied in Geneva with Piaget. In fact, the Americans and Elkind particularly, that were associated with him in Geneva have helped spread interest in Piaget's work in this country.

Piaget's Approach to Research

1. Piaget explored a number of traditional disciplines: biology, philosophy, and psychology, seeking one that would allow him to combine his philosophical interest in epistemology (that branch of philosophy concerned with how we gain knowledge) and his interest in biology and natural science. Piaget came to regard human intelligence—man's rational function—as providing the unifying principles of all the sciences including the social, biological, and natural disciplines. Some writers refer to Piaget as the most influential psychologyst of modern thought; others refer to him as an educator; some say he is neither. Piaget referred to himself as a genetic epistemologist, concerned with how children and adults gain knowledge and the change in the acquisition of knowledge over time. He tried to discover how the order and logic that characterizes rational thought evolves.

2. His methods of investigation, though derived from science and psychology, were in many respects uniquely Piagetian. When he first began his work, he studied the reasoning of young children as revealed in their games, in their questions, and in their responses to the verbal problems he posed to them. Later he spent hundreds of hours observing his own three children from birth onward, seeking evidence as to the emergence of the categories of object, space, causality, and time. From these investigations flowed a series of articles and books that are still among his most quoted.

3. Piaget has been criticized for the assumption that a detailed investigation of any small sample of the species will yield basic information inherent to all members of the species. He believed that children of Geneva, and his own particularly, were representative of children generally.[13]

4. Elkind believed the assertion that Piaget's studies were based on too few subjects was true only for his infancy investigation. In all other explorations, Piaget employed hundreds of subjects. He offers the following information in defense of Piaget's methods:
   a. His observations were intensive, sensitive, exceedingly detailed, recorded descriptions of behavior.
   b. With the aid of the student population, it was possible for Piaget and his graduate students to examine large numbers of children of all ages when they were conducting a particular research investigation.
   c. He would set up a problem and then for a year or more would pursue it intensely and without distraction.
   d. He met with his colleagues and graduate students once a week. At this time the possible ways of exploring the problem were discussed and data from ongoing studies presented. They were lively, exciting sessions in which new insights and ideas constantly emerged and served as stimuli for still further innovation.
5. Largely because of Piaget's influence, teacher training at Geneva University is heavily weighted in the direction of child development theory and research.
6. As a result of numerous investigations of children's conceptions of space, time, number, quantity, speed, causality, geometry, and so on, Piaget was able to arrive at a general conception of intellectual growth.
7. As Elkind pointed out, Piaget's contribution was infinitely more valuable than precisely controlled experiments. Piaget offered challenging ideas as an entry into new research.
   Bybee and Sund note this:

Throughout Piaget's career, he never failed to find uniqueness in the common, to lose sight of his purpose, and to find new problems to resolve. He lived a full and rich professional life and a personal life of continued actualization of his potentials.[3]

PIAGET'S THEORY OF ORGANIZATION AND ADAPTATION

Jean Piaget's theory is complex and contains several formidable obstacles.

1. The sheer volume and difficulty of Piaget's own writing causes problems.

2. His training and experience as a biologist influenced his theoretical formulations, the concepts of which are not always familiar to the psychology or child development student.

3. Students do not always understand the terminology used to describe various aspects of cognitive development.

4. Some students and writers approach his theory from developmental periods. This practice could produce a superficial knowledge of an extremely complicated system.

5. Without the understanding of his concepts of organization and adaptation, it is impossible to comprehend the range, depth, and richness of Piaget's cognitive theory.

The insights that Piaget offers are richly rewarding. Even though the ideas are difficult to comprehend, the extra work will be worth the effort, especially for those who will actually be in continuous contact with children as parents, teachers, nurses, or social workers.

An acquisition of factual knowledge of Piaget's theory allows one to relate to others on the basis of the level of their concept development. All involved will be able to blend this understanding with other theories that explain development and growth patterns in order to recognize what is is occurring in actual life situations.

Organization and Adaptation

Piaget believed that:

1. intelligence is the ability to organize and adapt to the environment.

2. since life is a continuous interaction between organism and environment, the interaction implies an external coping and an internal organization.[22]

3. organization constitutes the internal structure while adaptation is the basic tendency of the organism to use that structure to adjust to the environment. They are inherited biological factors in the sense that they are common to all species.

4. we constantly use these intellectual processes—organization and adaptation in all mental activities. They are a complementary aspect of a single process.

The following chart presents a skeletal framework of Piaget's theory of Organization and Adaptation in which the various entities are shown as different aspects of a single process. Organization and Adaptation are interwoven processes, and in life it is impossible to separate parts from the whole or to treat the whole separate from the parts. For clarification, however, each of Piaget's themes of organization and adaptation will be discussed separately while accepting and emphasizing the fact that they are all parts of a complementary, inseparable, biological, psychological process.

A Framework Of
Piaget's Theory Of Cognitive Development

ORGANIZATION	(Interwoven process)	ADAPTATION
(Internal structure)		(Interaction between internal structure and external stimuli)
STRUCTURE	CONTENT	FUNCTION
SCHEME, SCHEMATA OR SCHEMA		ASSIMILATION
Generic unit of structure, reflexes, mental operations, overt behavior, strategies, plans, transformations, experiences, series, classification, system of operations, connections, and groups		(Individual "interprets" environmental situations in terms of existing structures)
		ACCOMMODATION
		(Modifying of old schemes or building of new schemes)

EQUILIBRIUM OR EQUILIBRATION
(A striving for balance)

DISEQUILIBRIUM OR DISEQUILIBRATION
(Difference between cognitive structure and environmental stimulus)

Organization—Structure and Schemes

1. All manifestations of life, whatever they may be and at whatever level, give evidence of the existence of organization.[15]

2. Organization can be thought of as a basic inherited tendency for all species to systematize or organize their processes into coherent systems.

3. Just as there is a biological structure (e.g. a digestive system for the assimilation of food), there must be a mental structure to systematize stimuli and integrate actions, either motoric or cognitive, into coherent structures of a higher order to adapt to the world.[15]

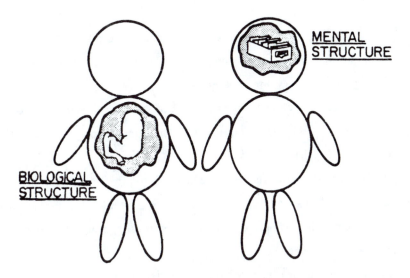

MENTAL STRUCTURE

BIOLOGICAL STRUCTURE

4. Intellectual development is a continual process of organization and reorganization of structures, each new organization integrating the previous one into itself. It is:

   a. a hierarcheal order within the structures;

   b. an open dynamic system with exchanges and interchanges within the structure upon contact with stimulus from the environment;

   c. a conceptual system whereby the elements are inevitably supported by one another while at the same time open to exchanges from the outer world;

   d. a circular system that allows for the extension of knowledge in an ever widening sphere as far as possible within its limits. The circular character gives organization another dimension in addition to the merely additive or linear concepts of knowledge.[15]

Cognitive Structures

1. Cognitive development consists of a succession of mental changes, and the changes are in the organizational structure. Cognitive structures are identifiable patterns of physical or mental action that underlie specific intelligence. Perhaps the best way to think of structure is to draw a parallel. The physical structure of the ear enables us to hear; the physical structure of the eye enables us to see; the psychological structures of the mind enable us to think and know. Just as the body has physical structures, so the mind has cognitive structures.[22]

2. The development of higher, more complex structures results from continuous adaptation to the environment.

3. The individual of any age must adapt to the environment and must organize his responses continually, but the instruments by which he accomplishes this—the psychological structures—will change from one level to another.[14]

4. Intellectual development proceeds through a series of stages with each stage characterized by a different kind of psychological structure: (1) sensorimotor, (2) preoperational, (3) concrete logical, and (4) formal logical.

5. The ability to differentiate perceptual input lends itself to intellectual development.

    a. The structure is only partially able to differentiate at the level of innate knowledge in infancy. It becomes increasingly complex with maturation, logical mathematical structures, and social exchanges.

    b. There is a difference in the structures ability to differentiate in higher and lower animals. The degree of differentiation made possible by the structural organ makes a difference in the way in which the animal kingdom and man adapts to the world.[12]

Schemes

1. Piaget uses the term scheme or schema (singular) and schemes or schemata (plural) interchangeably to refer to generic units of structure.

2. Schemes form a framework into which incoming sensory data can be processed and identified. A scheme is a mobile, fluid, cognitive structure that is created and modified by intellectual functioning. Any intelligent act, whether an infant's grasping an object or an adult's exercising an abstract judgement, is always related to the basic structure. It presupposes a basic organization. This basic structure is the schema—what is "generalizable" in a given action.[17]

74

3. Schemes are the cognitive structures by which:

   a. individuals intellectually adapt to and organize their world;

   b. events are organized as they are perceived by the organism into groups according to common characteristics;

   c. the overt behavior of the child is reflected.

4. Schemata are more than the behavior; they are the structure from which behavior flows. They are an inner representation of our activities and experiences.[24]

5. According to Piaget, "every schema is coordinated with all other schemata and itself constitutes a totality with differentiated parts."[19]

6. There is an interaction among schemes; they can assimilate each other.

7. The infant comes into the world equipped with a few hereditary reflexive schemata such as sucking and grasping.

   a. Repetitive experiences establish rhythm, sequential use, and a sense of order.

   b. The schemata of the newborn are the precursors of later mental activities.

   c. Increasingly complex schemata emerge out of the few reflexive schemata.

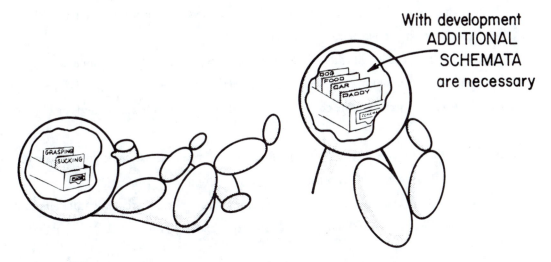

With development ADDITIONAL SCHEMATA are necessary

8. The older child's operational schemes are quite different from the infant's behavioral schemes. The infant acts overtly on the world. The older child's schemes involve mental operations.

9. The development of schemes involves activity on the part of the child. Piaget insists that:

   a. children must be allowed to do their own learning;

b. thought or "mental operations" emerge from motor action and sensory experiences;

c. to know an object means incorporating it into action schemata.

10. All activities reveal the existence of basic structural schemes, namely, the operation of:

    a. putting things together;

    b. placing them in classes;

    c. making series;

    d. making connections;

    e. making use of combination of "transformation groups."

11. According to Piaget, actions are not haphazard occurrences but rather:

    a. repeat themselves whenever similar situations arise;

    b. reproduce themselves exactly if there is the same interest in a similar situation;

    c. are differentiated and form a new combination if need or the situation alters.[16]

12. Physiological explanation:

There are some researchers who theorize the process of concept development from a physiological base. They hypothesize that:

    a. the neuron cells within the brain can be perfectly formed and yet inoperable unless the cells have been ignited electrically and biochemically;

    b. the only way the neuron cell can become ignited is through stimuli from the input system;

    c. a scheme to them would be a biochemically electrically charged neuron cell;

    d. from first-hand experiences the child builds an elaborate series of trace patterns or schemata;

    e. the stimulation from the input system lights up a series of neuron cells which then become the basis of future thought patterns;

    f. the input ignites a trace pattern, and that scheme or trace pattern crosses with others to bring to mind an array of thoughts, ideas, and experiences.

Content

1. Central to Piaget's theory are the concepts of cognitive structure, cognitive function, and cognitive content.

2. Cognitive content refers to the motoric or cognitive actions that are termed intelligent. The actions flow from the content of the schemes within the structure. They include:

   a. observable behaviors;

   b. problem-solving techniques;

   c. what the child or person says or does.

3. The totality of experiences shapes the interest and consequently the content of the individual and the specific experiences he tends to pursue.[13]

4. One simple aspect of thought is its manifest content. For instance, a mechanic is asked what makes a car go. The answer he gives is a reflection of the content of his thought. The content needed for adaptation by the mechanic would be different from the content needed by the teacher, the physician, or the lawyer. Profession then, to a degree, dictates content.[9]

5. The organizational content needed for adaptation depends on the environment, the cultural expectations, basic values, models, experiences, social interactions, and the learning history.[16]

6. The content needed to adapt to a simplistic society would not be adequate to adapt to a complex technological society.

7. Individuals achieve different levels of content within the hierarchy although, "there is in the brain of each individual the possibility for all these developments but they are not all realized."[19]

8. Piaget's major contentions are these:

   a. that each individual constructs his own reality;

   b. for each child this is a unique construction;

   c. the child, having the same general types of experiences available as everyone else, constructs his own content in terms of what the world is to him;

   d. knowing does not imply making a copy of reality but rather reacting to it and transforming it in such a way as to include it functionally in the transformation system with which these acts are linked.[13]

Reality for the child is never a mirror image of the real world. Children's content develops from limited information—unrefined, frequently inaccurate schemes—to increasingly more accurate and refined schemes.

Each child's content is a construction, not a copy of reality.

Adaptation
The Functional Process of Assimilation and Accommodation

1. For Piaget, intellectual adaptation is an interaction or an exchange between a person and his environment and involves two equally functional and important processes, (1) assimilation and (2) accommodation.

2. The cognitive functions of assimilation and accommodation do not change during development; they are, to use Piaget's term, "functional invariants," but they are responsible for changes in the cognitive organizational structure.

3. In any given situation that people interact with the environment, they cope as well as they can with the organizational structures or schemes that they have. The functional adaptation process of assimilation and accommodation allows them to modify the organizational structures and change their behavior to new and better patterns of response.

4. Piaget states that intelligence involves biological adaptation, equilibrium between the individual and his environment, and a set of mental operations which permit this balance.[9]

5. Adaptation is important for all living things because when an organism ceases to adapt to its environment, it simply dies.[12]

Assimilation

1. Assimilation is the process by which the person incorporates features of external reality into his own psychological structures. He deals with the environment in terms of his existing structural schemes.[24]

2. Assimilation is the taking-in process, whether by sensation, nourishment, or experience. It is the process by which one incorporates things, people, ideas, customs, and tastes into one's own activity.[24]

3. One assimilates an environmental event into existing intellectual structures or schemes.

4. No form of knowledge, not even perceptual knowledge, constitutes a simple copy of reality because it always includes a process of assimilation to previous structures.

5. Assimilation of motoric or cognitive actions is based on an underlying cognitive structure.

6. To say that all knowledge presupposes some assimilation and that it confers meaning amounts to saying that to know an object implies incorporating it into action schemata. This is true from elementary-sensorimotor behavior right up to the higher logico-mathematical operations.[16]

The child's first attempts to assimilate and accommodate are extremely imprecise and frequently inaccurate. For example, when a child experiences new things or sees old things in a new way, he tries to fit these new events or stimuli into the schemata he has at the time. When a child looks at a cat and says, "Dog," the child sifted through the schemata until he found one that seemed appropriate. To the child the object (cat) had all the characteristics of the dog. It was

small, furry, had four legs and fit into the dog schemata (the existing structure) so the child con-
cluded that the object was a dog. The stimulus (cat) was assimilated into the dog schemata.

Accommodation

1. Accommodation is the functional process of creation of new or the modification of existing
   schemata. It accounts for the change or development of new schemes.[24]
2. Accommodation refers to the organism's tendency to modify its structures according to the
   pressures of the environment, while assimilation involves using current structures.[9]
3. In the process of accommodating to the environment, the cognitive structures are expanded,
   broadened, or generalized so they incorporate increasingly larger and more accurate aspects
   of the world.
4. Assimilation is continuously balanced by accommodation; it is the outgoing, adjusting process
   of reaching out to the environment.
   a. Sometimes a stimulus cannot be placed or assimilated into a schema.
   b. The stimulus from the environment does not fit into the existing structure.
   c. Therefore, in order to achieve balance, one has to modify an old structure or build a new
      one so the stimulus can be assimilated.
   d. According to Piaget, it is easier to assimilate into existing structures than to modify or
      build new ones. Therefore, the process of accommodation is often accompanied by serious
      expression and thought.[20]

A New Stimulus—Dogs bark. Cat sounds different than dogs.

Disequilibrium—cat won't fit dog schema.

Cat schema is formed—therefore, accommodation.

5. Summary of the adaptive process of assimilation and accommodation:

    a. For Piaget, assimilation and accommodation are two sides of the adaptive coin. They can be separated for discussion, but they are inseparable in development.

    b. One assimilates an environmental event into a structure, and one accommodates a structure to the demands of the environment.

    c. Eventually the organism tends toward equilibrium. He aims toward a balance between his structure and the requirements of his world.[9]

Equilibrium and Disequilibrium

1. Piaget uses the terms equilibrium and disequilibrium to apply to a state of being or a feeling.

2. He uses the term equilibration and disequilibration to imply a process of active compensation set up by the subject against exterior disturbances.

3. Equilibrium's function is to bring about a balanced coordination between assimilation and accommodation.

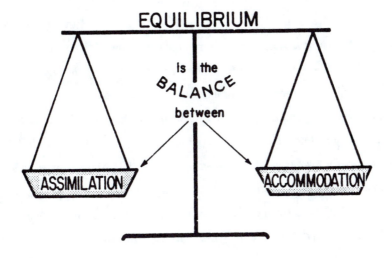

4. Intellectual development is an adaption or mental compensation in response to a discrepancy between the existing cognitive structure and a cognitive referent or stimulus in the environment.[16]

5. Equilibration represents the process of reconstructing the intellectual structure in order to incorporate the cognitive referent into the individual's organization.

6. Piaget recognizes that the emotions influence thought. In fact, he repeatedly states that no act of intelligence is complete without emotions. They represent the energetic or motivational aspects of intellectual activity. Disequilibrium is an emotional response and acts as a motivator to restore balance or equilibrium, a more comfortable feeling.[15]

7. It appears then, that a concept of moderate disequilibrium or mismatch is important for learning.

   a. It is a process that can be used by the classroom teacher because it is through the process of equilibration and disequilibration that learning takes place.

   b. In educational perspective, moderate disequilibrium is necessary for the resulting process of intellectual adaptation and thus a higher level of organization.

8. An example of Piaget's theory of organization and adaptation can be seen in students studying the theory for the first time.

   a. Students are assigned to read Piaget's basic theory.

   b. They encounter the terminology from the biological world, resulting in a disequilibrium between their mental structure and the referent or stimulus from the environment.

   c. They try to assimilate the terms into existing schemes, but find they do not have the structures which will allow them to assimilate the new concepts.

   d. When they were assigned to read Erikson's theory of the Eight Stages of Personality Development, they had not felt the same type of disequilibrium for they already had preexisting schemes for love, trust, doubt, shame, etcetera. The students existing schemes could be combined, assimilated, and joined with other schemes.

   e. To understand Piaget's theory, they have to accommodate by modifying old or building new schemes in order to assimilate. This experience involves a more serious thought process.

f. The students will need to change their organization by building larger, more inclusive intellectual structures so they can use this theory to adapt to new situations and process behavior in a more meaningful way.

g. If the disequilibrium or mismatch is too extreme, the students may simply withdraw from the situation by saying, "I don't want to know about Piaget's theory anyway."

h. According to Piaget, equilibrium is not an immediate state but a gradual progression from lesser to a more comfortable inclusive state.

i. As the students continue to explore, discover new applications, verbalize concepts, and receive additional information, they will gradually move toward a feeling of equilibrium. They will enjoy using Piaget's theory which will give them exciting new insights which can be used to adapt to their environment at a higher level.

9. Piaget states, "behavior is at the mercy of every possible disequilibrating factor since it is always dependent on an environment which has no fixed limits and is constantly fluctuating."[15]

BASIC ASSUMPTIONS
PIAGET'S COGNITIVE PERIODS OF DEVELOPMENT

Piaget, in relation to the four periods of cognitive development, believed that:

1. development follows a predictable pattern. Development is an epi-genetic process (one period is built upon another).

2. development is an inherent, unalterable, evolutionary process. It is gradual, continuous, and consistent.

3. with the development process there is a series of distinct developmental phases and sub-phases:

   a. Sensori-motor Intelligence (birth to two years).

   b. Preoperational Period (two to seven years).

   c. Concrete Operational Period (seven to eleven years).

   d. Formal Operational Period (eleven years throughout life).

4. each period is a pattern or organization which occurs in a definite sequence with an approximate age span in the continuium of development. At each stage, the child is involved in knowing the world through different modes and makes use of the different internal mechanisms for organization.

5. each child must pass through each stage before going on to a new, more complex one, and must pass through the stages in the same order.

6. age norms are approximate. Ages which children develop expected behavior are representative of a particular stage and are not fixed. Age spans are normative and only suggest the times which most children can be expected to display the intellectual behavior that is characteristic of that particular stage.

7. each stage sees the elaboration of new mental abilities which set the limit and determine the character of what can be learned at that period.

8. mental structures grow and develop from age to age. The structures of thought at each level are richer, more complex, and more inclusive.

9. each given stage is an integration of the one that preceded it. The achievement of that stage is a preparation for those that follow.

10. previous behavior patterns are thought of as inferior, and that perception becomes part of the new, superior level.

11. development proceeds from the simple to an ever-increasing complexity. The differences in organizational patterns create a hierarchy of experiences and actions.

12. individuals achieve different levels within the hierarchy.

13. progress is related to: (a) maturation, (b) physical experience, (c) social interaction, and (d) progression of equilibrium.

14. heredity can impede or facilitate intellectual functioning but cannot account for intellectual functioning by itself.

15. it is the specific nature of the physical and social environment of a culture that calls for the cognitive activity, and this nature determines both the rate and the extent of the development through the stages.

16. education can facilitate or impede development through the stages.

17. progression through the stages depends on the reorganization of mental structures which occurs when a person spontaneously acts on the environment (transforms it), experiences disequilibrium, and assimilates and accommodates events.[14]

18. Adaptation within each stage requires activity on the part of the individual. One cannot adapt at any level unless one acts.

PIAGET'S PERIODS OF COGNITIVE DEVELOPMENT

Sensorimotor Period of Development
(Birth to Approximately 2 Years)

Foundation of Intellectual Development

1. Piaget: The period that extends from birth to the acquisition of language is marked by an extraordinary development of the mind. The importance is sometimes underestimated because it is not accompanied by words that permit a step by step pursuit of the progress of intelligence and the emotions, as is the case later on. This early mental development, nonetheless, determines the entire course of psychological evolution. . . . At the starting point of this development, the neonate grasps everything . . . to his own body . . . whereas at the termination of the period, i.e. when language and thought begin, he is . . . in a universe that he has gradually constructed himself, and which hereafter he will experience as external to himself.

2. Piaget believed that the very foundation of intelligence is established during the first years of life. The primary task of the period is the acquiring and using of elementary capacities that will later become intelligent thought.

3. Piaget did not pose an outer reality for the infant; he saw construction of reality as the infant's basic task.

The Sensorimotor Period

1. The first stage of mental development, the sensorimotor period, is called this because a child interacts with the environment through the senses and motoric activity. The infant increasingly senses stimuli (sensory reaction) and responds by moving muscles (motoric reaction).

2. The infant's world is restricted essentially to practical interaction with objects within the immediate environment which are linked to physical satisfaction, an activity which contributes to the development of intelligence.[11]

3. To the infant, time is now. Infants neither think of the past nor the future. They function only in the present for they do not have mental images.

4. Space involves only that which surrounds him and is limited to the immediate area.

5. The infant is locked in egocentrism; the baby is unaware of anything beyond himself. He cannot at first distinguish himself from the world and is confused about the difference between self and other objects. Increasingly, the active child experiences the world and he begins to understand that he may control his own actions. By twelve months the infant is able to differentiate between self, others, and objects.

Reflexive Actions

1. Throughout most of the first month, the behavior of the infant is largely reflexive; that is the infant responds to the world largely in terms of the reflexes he is born with (e.g. crying, grasping, sucking, and specific movements of head, trunk, legs and arms).
2. The infant does not have mental images so must process the world only through the senses. Behavior patterns involving seeing, smelling, tasting, hearing, touching, and manipulating are used during this period to gain knowledge of the world.[11]
3. According to Piaget, the infant is active rather than passive and seeks contact with the environment. Infant curiosity does not wait for environmental events to happen but seeks increased levels of stimulation and excitation. When some environmental event occurs, the infant does not register it passively but instead interprets it and gradually constructs his own reality.[9]
4. Reflexes are the basis of what will later be intelligent action. By having numerous similar physical experiences, the infant begins to organize the grasping and sucking ability. He begins building and combining basic schemes and slowly begins the process of assimilation and accommodation.

Intentionality to Goal Directed Behavior

1. Reflexive schemes are strengthened through repeated use.
2. Repetitive actions develop and the child repeatedly hits a toy hanging from his crib (habitual actions).
3. The infant gradually begins to initiate intentional goals (directed behavior).
    a. The baby kicks his bed and the mobile overhead moves and makes a noise. He moves around and explores until he kicks and it moves and makes a noise again.
    b. The child manipulates objects (e.g. pulls toys toward him by pulling the blanket they are on).

c. The child cries and his mother picks him up. The child cries again so his mother will pick him up.

4. The infant gradually moves from reflexive schemes to repetitive actions, to intentional coordination of actions and goal-directed behavior, to what Piaget terms practical intelligence.

Imitation, Play and Language

1. Imitation of infant's own behavior (1–4 months)
   a. The infant repeats and imitates his own reflexive actions.
   b. If the adult repeats or imitates the infant's "gooing" and "cooing" sounds, the infant will repeat or imitate the gestures and sounds of the adult.

2. Imitation of adult behavior (4–12 months)
   a. If the adult bangs a pan with a spoon, the infant will imitate the action and bang the pan.
   b. If the adult claps his hands and says, "patty cake, patty cake," the infant will clap his hands in imitation.
   c. This is called immediate imitation and depends on the adult being present.

3. Deferred imitation and play (12 months–2 years)
   a. The child begins imitating remembered actions.
      (1) The infant picks up a toy telephone, holds the telephone as an adult would and makes babbling sounds into the phone.
      (2) The adult does not have to be present for this type of deferred imitation.
   b. The infant is forming rudiments of representational thought which will manifest itself more clearly in the preoperational stage. The infant can engage in play through a remembered situation.

4. Beginning of language
   a. At the end of the sensorimotor period, children demonstrate they are capable of simple play and imitation.
   b. They may act out a role or experiment with symbolic play as in language.
   c. Imitation and representational thought lend themselves to the symbolic process of the beginnings of language.
   d. According to Piaget, first comes the sensorimotor exploration, then play and imitation, and then the simple word.

Object Permanence

1. Up to a given age, in the six-to-eight month range, it seems that the baby is totally unaware that an object continues to exist after it has passed from view. The baby watches intently as a plaything is slowly put under a blanket. The moment the object disappears, the baby's expression goes blank and its eyes drift elsewhere. There is no sign of surprise or bewilderment, and the baby makes no effort to try to locate the vanished object. Out of sight is out of mind.

2. The acquisition of object permanence, the realization that objects continue to exist even though they can no longer be seen, is not an abrupt, all-or-nothing matter. It develops gradually. There are certain privilege "objects", such as the parents, that take on permanence long before other, less emotion-charged things. The three-month-old screaming in protest against having been put to bed in the evening seems fully aware that the parents are still there.[21]

3. A four-month-old is able to retrieve a toy that is only partially hidden; if the toy is completely covered, of course, the child loses interest.

4. As permanence develops, beginning around seven or eight months, the vanished object will continue to exist for the baby, but only in a fixed location.

5. At the next stage, the baby can watch a plaything being moved from one hiding place to another and looks in the place where the object made its final disappearance.

6. By late infancy, babies can hide a plaything under or behind a couch or in a closet and then retrieve it a day or so later, indicating **permanency,** linked with location.

7. **Object permanence** is a significant advancement because permanent objects help the child deal with reality.

Summary—The Sensorimotor Child

1. The sensorimotor child spans a tremendous cognitive distance in two years.
2. The infant grows from a *reflex dominated* creature to a *dynamic, functioning child.*
3. The *active child* has adapted and learned how to obtain satisfaction thereby demonstrating to some degree intelligent *intentional* behavior.
4. The infant has advanced from being able to make slight *discriminations* to *identifying objects, places,* and *people.*

5. The infant has developed a primitive notion of *causality,* for he has discovered that certain actions of his produce certain results.

6. The infant has achieved the notion of *object constancy*—the realization that objects and people have a permanent existence which is independent of his perception of them.

7. The infant, by experimenting with objects, has acquired *rudimentary concepts of space* and *time.* He can locate his toys and knows that daily events have a certain sequence.

8. The infant experiences himself now as one among many and understands himself as a *single entity.* His discovered awareness of himself as separate from other people decreases his *egocentrism.*

9. He has left the crib to become involved and experiment in play by acting out roles and *imitating models.*

10. His *motoric patterns* are slowly being replaced by *semi-mental* functionings.

11. The infant is now capable of moving intellectually into the *preoperational stage.*

Implication and Application

1. Development results from an interaction between infant and environment.

2. The infant should be stimulated through objects and events, for this facilitates the continual transformation of basic structures.

3. The infant should be allowed to explore the world, for actions contribute to the construction of reality.[3]

Preoperational Period
(Approximately 2–7 Years)

Development from Reflexes to Mental Operations

1. Toward the end of the second year the child progresses from the reflexive sensorimotor actions of infancy to a new cognitive or mental process—symbolic representation.

2. The child now functions intellectually with mental images. Children this age have the ability to make something—a mental symbol, a word, or an object—stand for or represent something else.

3. The ability to symbolize makes it possible for the child to operate on new intellectual levels. The use of symbols frees the child from infancy dependence on the immediate environment. He can now recall past events, project future ones, and communicate internal states to others.

4. Evidence of the mental development during the preoperational stage is seen in the form of imitation, symbolic play, symbolic drawing, and language. Other indicators of symbolic representation are found in dreams and nightmares.

5. Piaget divided preoperation thought into two stages:

   a. Preconceptual thought occurs at approximately two to four years of age in which the child's actions are mediated by representational thought (i.e., signs, symbols, and mental images). During this stage a child's concerns are associated with the development of language. The world can be symbolized, imagined; recalled actions can be imitated, deferred, and explained.[13]

   b. Intuitive stage occurs at approximately four to seven years of age. Intuitive means the power of knowing at once without conscious reasoning. The child explains problems in a prelogical manner. The child's intuitive answers indicate a partial coordination of actions or patterns of thought. The child can only partially complete mental operations because he cannot reverse actions. Preoperational children cannot reason about their thinking, and they are incapable of analyzing, synthesizing, and evaluating thoughts.[23]

6. Piaget refers to the period as preoperational.

   a. "Pre" means "before."

   b. "Operation" means "mental action."

   c. Therefore, preoperational is the period before a child can perform mental operations or reason logically.

7. The preoperational child makes such an intellectual leap forward from the sensorimotor stage that it is sometimes difficult to realize how elementary their thinking still is.

Language

1. Piaget argues that language does not fully shape the child's mental activities. Despite his new ability at language, the child often thinks non-verbally. A child's thoughts depend less on his language than his language depends on his thoughts.

2. According to Piaget, language development occurs only after the child becomes capable of internal representation. At the beginning of this stage the child tends to identify words and symbols with the objects they are intended to represent. The typical toddler is constantly asking, "Whatzat?" They are asking for words or symbols to identify objects.

3. Children interpret words in terms of their own personal system of meaning, and the child's meaning is not necessarily the same as the adult's. The child distorts the language to fit his own mental structures.[9]

4. During the first half of the preoperational period, from the age of two to four, the extremely rapid development of spoken language occurs. By four years of age the average child in any culture has mastered much of his or her native language. Typically he or she understands and uses a great number of words and uses the main body of the language's grammar effectively. Children this age can now use fairly complex sentence structures.

5. During the preoperational period, part of the child's language is communicative and the other part is non-communicative or egocentric. Children often engage in monologues, collective monologues, repetitive statements, and dialogues. Even though there is language, at times there is not much communication.

6. The language preschool children use gives us insight into the structure of their cognitive and emotional functioning. Language and representation help make preoperational thought much more efficient and powerful than it was during the sensorimotor period. Thinking through language takes less time than thinking through action.[23]

Play, Imitation and Make-Believe

1. According to Piaget, play is one of the most important functions of childhood. It is a vehicle for total development. He argues eloquently for recognizing its importance in a youngster's life. Children are obliged to adapt themselves to social and physical worlds that they only slightly understand and appreciate. The child must make intellectual adaptations that leave personality needs unmet. For their mental health, they must have some outlet, some technique that will permit them to assimilate reality to self, and vice versa. Children find this mechanism in play.[17]

2. Play helps the child overcome egocentrism. Through repeated social interaction, another individual's needs, interests, and goals can come into focus for a child.

3. Play and imitation are an important part of Piaget's theory. He feels that play is almost pure assimilation without any attempt to adapt to outer reality. Imitation is the child's serious attempt to accommodate to outer reality. The give and take in play and imitation is one way that the child learns about the world.[20]

4. Play bridges the gap between sensorimotor experience and the emergence of representative or symbolic thought.

Egocentrism

1. Egocentrism is the degree to which a child views himself as the center of reality. Preoperational children are quite egocentric.

2. The child knows the world only as he sees it; he knows no alternatives. He sees his physical and social world only as he has previously experienced them. This limited view of things leads to his assumption that everyone thinks as he does and understands him without his having to work to convey his thoughts and feelings.[9]

3. This egocentricity is not selfishness or even inconsideration when it manifests itself in anti-social behavior. It is not a conscious behavior but rather an inability to take into account the interests of others, not realizing that they may differ from his own.

4. The child assimilates incoming stimuli to his own schemes rather than accommodating to the schemes of others.

Number, Space, Time and Causality

1. Time

   a. The preoperational child's concept of time has broadened since the sensorimotor stage. The child now thinks not only in terms of the present but can recall yesterday and think of tomorrow.

   b. The child's extension of time, however, is limited to short periods not too distant from the present. Clock time ordinarily eludes the preschool child except for those hours that mark turning points in the day's activities.

   c. Designations of time gradually become more precise during this period and many children may know the days of the week, the seasons of the year, and some of the main holidays that fall in different seasons.

d. Having adults structure time into dependable but unhurried schedules and routines helps the preschool child gain a sense of reoccurrences, stability, and predictability.

2. Space

   a. In infancy and toddlerhood, spatial relations are linked to the child's own actions and migrations; they function in what is called action space. The very young child has no notion of how things and places are located relative to one another.[21]

   b. The preschool child moves gradually from action space into what is called map space in which the locations of objects are linked into an overall mapped pattern. Not until the late preschool or early school years are children able to form a mental map.

   c. The child's concept of space has also broadened from the immediate area in which he interacts with the house, yard, and the neighborhood. However, the understanding of larger geographic space such as state, country, and world is still very limited.

3. Number and Quantity

   a. The child of this period does not truly understand the significance of number. He may know how to count but he doesn't comprehend the cardinal and ordinal meaning of numbers. He knows the names of numbers but not their significant properties.[2]

   b. He has highly unstable notions of number and of quantity in general. When asked to compare two rows of pennies in terms of equality or unequality of number, the children are guided by the length of the rows more than by the number of pennies each row contains.

   c. In conservation (sameness) of quantity tasks, children perceive the same lump of clay as changing in bulk when it is rolled into a sausage or cut in two.

4. Causality

   a. Young children do not inquire closely into causation but seem to accept cause and effect as a given. They simply seem to take events for granted without wondering for a moment what makes things happen. Thus the sun sets so that we can have night, or we have night so that we can sleep.

   b. *Animism.* The child is animistic as he views phenomena and objects such as rocks, wind, blocks, and dishes as though they were alive and had psychological and logical attributes. He becomes angry because the toy block left on the stair tripped him.

c. *Artificialism*. The child assumes a human creation to everything. When a little boy was asked why there were two mountains above Geneva, he said the big one was made for big people to climb and the little one was made for children to climb.[20]

d. *Realism*. The young child regards his own perspective as immediate, objective, and absolute. To him all things are equally real—words, pictures, dreams, and feelings. He has trouble differentiating between reality and fantasy. A three year old boy, Aron, cried each night when his mother put him to bed because there was a green monster in the closet that ate little boys.

Moral Development

1. The young preoperational child assumes that the rules of good and bad, right and wrong, have their own existence as part of the natural order.

2. The young child has no notion that moral rules are human inventions and conventions, but attributes to them the same solidity, permanence, absoluteness, and inescapability common to all the other forces of nature.

3. He believes that misdeeds carry within them the seeds of their own punishment, that the seriousness of wrongdoing is to be judged strictly in terms of the seriousness of the outcome with no allowance made for motives or extenuating circumstances. Piaget has made up a number of stories to test this tendency. For instance, the child who breaks a dozen dishes trying to help an ailing parent is judged more harshly than one who breaks a single dish while trying to raid the family money jar.

4. Kindergarten (and older) children distinguish quite clearly between acts leading to personal injury and those leading merely to property damage; children can take intentions into account.

Identity

1. Identification evolves from imitation. First, individuals become cognizant of the worth (to them) of the person to be imitated, then of the model's imitatable characteristics.

2. Investing a model with unusual desirability and/or power leads to identification. Piaget explains this emergence: The child feels close to those who satisfy his immediate needs and interests. He selects them as his model. These spontaneously selected models become the measuring stick for value judgements for years and remain the object of identification and

obedience. Under ordinary conditions the young child maintains a sense of respect and awe for the superior powers of his caretakers. He places them in an omnipotent positions. The child's sense of obedience and awe . . . is derived from a combination of love and fear and provides the foundation of his conscience.[19]

3. These experiences of identification become guideposts for judgement. With an increased capacity for refined differentiation of effect, children build up their system of values, their conscience. Identification is also strengthened by the child's accommodation to the pressure of the environment.[13]

Preoperational Thought

Although we see the steady development of thought during this period, there are still some limitations to preoperational thought. As the name "preoperation" implies, this period comes before advanced symbolic operations develop. Piaget claims that knowledge is not just a mental image of an object or event. To know an object is to act on it, to modify it, to transform it, and to join objects in a class. The preoperational child lacks the ability to perform such operations on concepts and objects.[17]

Blocks to Logical Thought

1. *Centration.* When the child is presented with a visual stimulus, he tends to center or fix his attention on a limited perceptual aspect of the stimulus. The child is incapable of thinking in terms of the whole. He is preoccupied with the parts. If he attempts to think in terms of the whole, he loses sight of the parts and their relationships which he is just beginning to grasp.

2. *Transformation.* The child, while observing a sequence of changes of successive states, focuses exclusively on the elements in the sequence, or successive states rather than on the transformation by which one state is changed to another. He does not focus on the process of transformation from an original state to a final state, but restricts his attention to each in-between state when it occurs.

3. *Reversibility.* To think logically, the child needs to have the ability to follow the line of reasoning back to where it started. Only when actions become reversible will the child be able to solve problems. The inability to reverse operations is seen in all cognitive activity of the preoperational child.

An example of the preceeding three blocks to logical thought: Piaget used two sticks or two pencils of equal length.

1. "Are the pencils the same length?" Child, "Yes."

   _____

   _____

2. "Are the pencils the same length?" Child, "No." "Is one longer than the other?" Child: "Yes."

   _____

   _____

3. "Are the pencils the same length?" Child, "Yes."

   _____

   _____

Explanation: The child's attention was centered or fixed on one aspect; he could not follow the transformation from one state to another nor could he reverse the action to reason that the pencils were the same length in the beginning so they were still the same length.

4. *Conservation.* This is the conceptualization that the amount or quantity of a matter stays the same regardless of any change in shape or position. The preoperational child's development from non-conservation to conservation is a gradual one.

   Example of the above: When Piaget filled two low, round glasses with water, the preoperational child said they each had the same amount of water. When he poured one of the glasses of water into a tall, thin glass, the child said the tall, thin glass contained more water.

Classification and Seriation

1. Piaget believed that certain mental abilities underlie the logical thought processes characteristic of older children and adults. These primary abilities include classification or grouping and seriation or ordering things according to their relative dimensions. These processes will provide valuable foundations for the construction of later mental skills needed by children in elementary school. The gradual development of such abilities underlies progression from preoperational stage to that of concrete operations and helps children move through blocks to logical thought wherein children become capable of more advanced logico-mathematical reasoning.[20]

96

2. Classification. Older children can form hierarchial classes and/or classify items according to number of properties at the same time. Preoperational children can perform at a simpler level; four and five year olds are able to sort objects or pictures into categories that are meaningful to them. Two and three year olds are able to perceive the concept of sameness and differences and match things that are not too detailed. Teachers and adults need to systematically and regularly provide opportunities for practice of these mental abilities.[10]

3. Seriation or Ordering. This is the arranging of objects or events in a logical order. The two kinds of ordering that appear to be most useful are arranging a variety of items according to a graduated scale (spatial ordering) and arranging events as they occur in time (temporal ordering). The basic question that the child must be able to answer when dealing with either of these concepts is, "What comes next?" Two and three year olds do best when a chain of two or three items is used. Preschool children can manage several.

4. Margaret Boden in her book, *Jean Piaget*, states that Piaget insists that before understanding can be internalized linguistically it must exist in practical form. A young child who says, "two and two are four," or who does the sum in figures, does not yet know or understand cardinal numbers or understand the equivalence of sets. The child has to discover or construct the realization that two dolls need two hats. The child has yet to construct the scheme or ordinal number, which assures that it is the medium-size doll who gets the medium-size hat. The relevant intellectual structures are developed through the child's own activities of comparing, ordering, matching, grouping, and sorting physical objects and bodily actions. So a child who the traditionalist might see as "just playing with beads" is spontaneously developing abstract structures such as the schemes of seriation and classification, which in their later operational form will organize logico-mathematical thinking in general.[2]

Summary—The Preoperational Child

1. The preoperational child has moved from reflexive sensorimotor actions to *symbolic representation*.

2. The child has made tremendous strides in *language development*.

3. He delights in *play* and *imitation*, a process of assimilation and accommodation.

4. He is *egocentric* and feels the world thinks as he thinks.

5. The child can think in terms of *present, past,* and *future* but distant time and clock time still elude him.

6. The child functions in *action space* and is gradually moving into *map space.*

7. The child does not truly understand the significance of *number.*

8. He attributes lifelike characteristics to innate objects—*animisn;* he assumes a human creation to everything and regards his own perspective as absolute—*artificialism.*

9. The child takes *cause and effect* as a given and for granted.

10. He has no notion that *moral rules* are human inventions and judges wrongdoing by the outcome rather than the intention.

11. He *identifies* with significant models.

12. The preoperational child cannot perform *logical mental operations* because of certain *blocks to logical thought.*

13. He can perform simple *classification* and *seriation* tasks.

Implication and Application

Parents and teachers need to:

1. provide an enriched environment.

2. give children opportunities to be actively involved in their own learning by exploring, discovering, and manipulating their world.

3. be good language models; encourage children to talk, and listen carefully to what children have to say. Language is a good indicator of the schemes they have to function with.

4. understand developmental stages and be able to assess their cognitive development using Piagetian tasks.

5. understand the interwoven relationship between physical, emotional, moral, social, and intellectual development.

6. be careful not to push children beyond their cognitive level. Children think with their brains, they can only think with the neural connections that they have developed at that particular time. Hurrying a child through a stage will not speed up brain growth. It will only deprive a child of the proper experiences needed for stimulation.[2]

7. realize that early reading and math skills are not accurate indicators of intellectual ability.[2]

Concrete Logical Operational Period
(Approximately 7 — 11 Years)

From Preconceptual Intuitive Thought to Concrete Logical Operations

1. The preoperational child made tremendous strides intellectually in symbolic thought processes but was still limited by intuitive thought and could not perform logical mental operations. A major cognitive shift takes place between the preschool and school years, and the child between the ages of seven and eleven or twelve years of age gradually moves toward the performance of mental operations.

2. During the period of concrete operations, the child's reasoning processes become more logical. That is, the child evolves logical thought processes (mental operations) that can be applied to concrete problems. They are freed from the pull of immediate perception, but in spite of this new freedom they are only capable of thought about concrete, existing objects and people. They cannot deal with complex verbal or hypothetical problems. They cannot think abstractly.

3. Mental processes are now incorporated into coherent systems. Thought patterns follow a set of logical rules. They use their minds to check the reasonableness of something rather than just relying on perception. This marks the difference between the practical concrete student and the intuitive child.

4. The concrete operational child learns best through exploration and manipulation of his environment; consequently, the period is sometimes referred to as a period of "hands-on learning."

Concrete Logical Reasoning Strategies

1. Decentration. The child now has the ability to stand back from a situation and take note of several features and their interrelationships instead of focusing on only one aspect at a time.

2. Conservation. Middle years children realize that altering the shape of material does not modify the amount present. Children through their interaction with materials in the environment gradually develop a conceptual understanding of conservation. When confronted with the changing shape of the clay balls, they know that nothing has been either added to or taken from something, it has to stay the same quantitatively.

3. Reversibility. The ability to reverse operations, to take something back to the original state, is accomplished in the concrete period, thus allowing the child to operate mentally. For instance, subtraction reverses addition and division reverses multiplication.

4. Transition. Another aspect of concrete-operational thought is transivity, the ability to follow a process and understand the relationship between successive stages. When the child is confronted with the pencil task, he will be able to follow the movement of one pencil being placed ahead of the other pencil.

Language

1. At the heart of the school child's cognitive status is increasing mastery of symbols. Preschool children are trapped in word realism, making it hard for them to sort out the false from the true. Concrete operational children have usually mastered some of the key fundamentals of language. The cognitive status of school children depends largely on their grasp of symbols which helps them to outgrow verbal realism.

2. Middle years children have begun to sense that words and the things they supposedly refer to belong to distinct levels of reality. This differentiation of levels gives children a new freedom to manipulate symbols, as seen in the delight they take in playing with words and meanings. Middle years children typically are fascinated by rhymes, codes, ciphers, anagrams, words and phrases, and the dual meaning of puns.

Egocentrism

1. The concrete operational child is not egocentric as the preoperational child is egocentric. He is aware that others can come to conclusions that are different from his. He comes to seek validation of his thoughts.

2. Liberation from egocentrism comes about primarily through social interaction with peers.

3. Egocentrism for the concrete operational child takes the form of being free from immediate perceptions, but limited to concrete, tangible problems of the present. The child cannot deal with complex hypothetical, verbal problems.

4. Middle years children are better judges of what other people know, think, and feel than are preschool children. However, there are marked individual differences between both children and adults in the ability to take account of other people's viewpoints.

Play, Imitation and Make-Believe

1. Through play the child's contact with the physical world becomes more productive. The assimilation and accommodation process expands and the child develops schemes for the skills required to use the tools and toys and play the games of the culture.

2. Children this age play games with rules which are essentially social, leading to increased adaptation. Piaget feels that the preschool child's imitative and make-believe play dies out in these years in favor of socialized games.

3. What happens to fantasy, the lovely private world of make-believe, when preoperational childhood is left behind? Piaget suggests that some of it is "interiorized" in daydreams and much of it goes to enrich developing intellectual interests. Creative imagination does not diminish with age but is gradually reintegrated in intelligence.

4. Imitation.

   a. Emancipation from parental dominance and greater participation in the social world bring about a shift in the child's models of imitation.

   b. Observations, comparisons, and comprehension of others assume an important part in the life of children.

Moral Development

1. The younger child's moral attitude of equating wrong-doing with consequences is subject to change, and the concrete operational child takes into account the motives of others and judges them more realistically. Piaget believes that moral judgement shifts from an objective orientation to a subjective orientation.

2. Children from ages seven to eleven generally become more interested in the rules which regulate their lives.

3. The child's awareness of social reciprocity and equality carries over to the concepts of fairness and justice. "It's not fair," is one of the battle cries of this age.

4. Equality in punishment, exact compensation for the damage done, and doing to another exactly what was done to oneself are conceived as fair judgements. Moral judgement among children is far more stringent than among adults.

5. During the middle years, focus of control generally moves from the external toward the internal. Conscience finds its anchoring points in newly acquired centers of mutual respect and an awareness of necessity for collective social obedience.[21]

Time, Space and Causality

1. Time

   a. Middle years children begin to locate themselves in time. They realize the world existed before they entered it and that it will survive their passing.

   b. They learn about clock and calendar time and begin to schedule their activities.

   c. They meditate about what it means to be age ten or twelve or twenty.

   d. They become able to think about things distant in time and space. They are fascinated with some historical episodes and have some ideas of their place in time.

2. Space

   a. The concrete student's conceptual understanding of space has broadened to include mental maps and some notions of geographical space.

   b. They can think of the area of city, state, and country and have some notion of place in terms of miles, hours, and distance.

   c. They turn their attention toward the world at large.

3. Causality

   a. Concrete operational children want to know about the mechanics of things—how they work and how they are made.

   b. They still enjoy fantasy but know that they are fantasizing.

   c. In dealing with means and ends, children discover the consequences one part has for another.

   d. Systematic comparison and independent measurements of events and things bring into the foreground a more realistic appraisal of the physical world.

   e. They realize that dreams are perceived only by the dreamer and that they are in the head.

   f. They become intrigued by the world of nonhuman nature such as animals, plants, rock formations, planets, stars, the moon, and the sun.[21]

Classification, Seriation and Number

1. Classification

    a. In the concrete operational period children develop the ability to categorize objects in three different aspects: simple classification, multiple classification, and class inclusion. Each class represents a different, more complex expression of the ability to categorize objects, persons, or situations.

    b. During the concrete operational period, children usually realize that a major class may be composed of sub-classes and that these in turn may belong to other groups.

    c. Children construct ascending and descending hierarchies as part of class inclusion. Children come to realize that sub-groups may belong to major groups. The child realizes that roses are flowers, roses have petals, and so do flowers.

    d. During the concrete operational period, children usually realize that a major class, dog for example, may be composed of subclasses such as little dogs, and that these in turn may belong to other groups such as color, or brown dogs.[3]

2. Seriation

    a. Seriation is the ability to arrange things in a sensible order such as arranging a set of rods according to increasing or decreasing length.

    b. Piaget points out that the scheme of seriation is an essential component for many of the complex types of scientific reasoning including the understanding of number (to which class inclusion also contributes).

    c. Middle years children master such arbitrary series as the alphabet and such logical ones as the number series. Not only can they count indefinitely, they can figure out the rules of a complex series.

    d. Children develop a systematic, coordinated method of seriating that reflects a completely developed seriation structure.

3. Number

    a. Development and conservation of the number concept is interconnected with seriation and classification. There is a synthesis of class inclusion and seriation in the development of number concepts.

    b. For a child to truly understand number, he must first be able to represent mentally how many objects are involved, order them, and classify them.

c. The concrete operation student begins to unfold in his ability to perform mathematical operations. By the end of the concrete period, the child is able to add, subtract, multiply, divide, place in order, substitute and reverse.[23]

Summary—The Concrete Logical Child

1. The concrete logical child moves intellectually from intuitive thought process to *mental concrete operations.*
2. He can *decentrate, conserve, reverse action,* and *follow a transition.*
3. He moves toward an increasing *mastery* of *symbols* and has the freedom to manipulate them as he *plays* with *words* and meanings.
4. The concrete child is not *egocentric* as the preoperational child is. This child is aware that others can come to conclusions that are different from his. He is *limited* to *concrete, tangible problems* of the present.
5. The child's *play* is *"interiorized"* in daydreams and enriches intellectual interests and creative thought.
6. He *shifts models* of *imitation.*
7. He moves from *external* to *internal moral conscience.*
8. The child can locate himself in *time,* and learns about *clock, calendar,* and *historical time.*
9. The child wants to know about the *mechanics of things—how they work* and how they are made.
10. The concrete logical child moves from *simple classification* to *multiple classification* and *class inclusion.*
11. He masters series as the *alphabet* and *number series.*
12. By the end of the concrete period, he can *add, subtract, multiply, divide, place in order, substitute,* and *reverse.*

Implication and Application

Teachers need to:

1. Plan teaching Strategies based on concrete experiences.
2. Present situations that are familiar to students.

3. Provide activities at all levels where students can interact on an individual basis with objects. Give them a chance to create their own mental structures.

4. Remember that chronological age is not an accurate means of determining a child's development. Responses to Piagetian tasks will provide a much more accurate indication of reasoning abilities.

5. Match the instruction to the individual child's needs.

6. Give children opportunities to think and develop reasoning and problem-solving abilities.

7. Understand that memorization and regurgitation does not indicate intellectual reasoning power.

Formal Logical Operations Period
(Approximately 11—15 Years)

From Sensorimotor to Formal Logical

1. At first, during the sensorimotor stage, there is the development of knowledge through physical action.

2. During the second, or preoperational stage, the child develops symbols to represent things that are not present. Thought is prelogical and is best described as intuitive.

3. In the next stage, concrete operational, the student's thought is logical but confined to practical experiences.

4. Finally in the formal operational stage, the adolescent demonstrates logical patterns of reasoning about abstract ideas and problems. The student demonstrates reflexive thought.

Structure

1. The adolescent's cognitive structures have now developed to the point where they can effectively adapt to a great variety of problems. The structures are sufficiently stable to assimilate readily a variety of novel situations.

2. This does not mean that the adolescent's growth ceases at age sixteen. He has much to learn in many areas. Piaget maintains that by the end of adolescence, the individual's way of thinking—that is, his cognitive structures—are almost fully formed. While these structures may be applied to new problems with the result that significant knowledge is achieved, the structures themselves undergo little modification after adolescence.[18]

3. Piaget agrees with others that it is conceivable that neurological development occurs around the time of puberty and provides the basis for the appearance of formal operations. He does not feel that neurological change provides a sufficient explanation, however, for there are cultures whose members lack formal operations. He believes that social interaction, the child's own activity and experience, education, and total environment also play a role.

Formal Logical Operations

1. Unlike the concrete child, the youth becomes an individual who thinks beyond the present and forms theories about everything, delighting especially in consideration of that which is unlikely.[11]

2. Mental operation, or acts of thought, are completed on situations and information that have not, or may not even occur. Mental action no longer requires actual objects, events, or situations. Adolescents can transcend the immediate here and now, can deal with abstract concepts and verbal propositions.

3. The adolescent acquires the capacity to think beyond his own realistic world and his own beliefs and can deal efficiently with the complex problems of reasoning.

4. The adolescent is concerned with what could be while the concrete child is concerned with what is. He uses propositions rather than sole reality, deals with relativity, balance and equality between concepts, actions and reactions.

5. Adolescents can conceive of themselves as wholly separate entities apart from their families, friends, institutions, and communities. This can be frightening; as a separate entity, they may feel isolated and vulnerable. At the same time, however, this new awareness of self holds out enormous possibilities. As never before, the adolescent can now plan his own life, assume responsibility for his own fate, consider all possibilities in career, personal life-style, and systems of belief.[8]

Theoretical and Hypothetical Thought

1. In the concrete period conservation, class inclusion, ordering, and reversibility are characteristic reasoning patterns. In the formal period, theoretical propositional, hypothetical, and combinational reasoning patterns are characteristic. The individual is able to carry on a whole

series of logical mental processes using mental operations. He can hold a large body of information in his mind and manipulate it mentally.

2. The adolescent develops the ability to imagine the possibilities inherent in a situation. Before acting on a problem which confronts him, he can analyze it and attempt to develop hypotheses concerning what might occur. These hypotheses are numerous and complex because the adolescent takes into account all possible combinations of eventualities in an exhaustive way. As he proceeds to test his ideas, he designs experiments which are quite efficient in terms of supporting some hypotheses and disproving others.[9]

3. The student can reason with alternate hypotheses, musing over the possible and probable as well as the abstract and concrete. He has the capacity to combine all variables and find a solution to a problem. He speculates on the effect of one variable on another and combines and separates variables in a hypothetical, deductive fashion.

4. He is no longer bound by actual occurrences and data from the sensory world. He is free to jump from proposition to proposition and from hypothesis to hypothesis to gain insight into behavior by combining theories.

5. Because of the significant advances in operational ability during this period, formal thinkers are capable of understanding, constructing, and applying abstract theories. Theoretical reasoning enables the individual to interact more effectively with the environment.

Time, Space, Symbols, Mathematics and Science

1. Time and Number

   a. The understanding of time and space increases significantly for the adolescent student. He thinks of distant places and larger and larger units of space. He also imagines long periods of time. He grasps the meaning of infinity, historical time, global geography, and interplanetary space.

   b. He can conceive of both present and future problems caused by changes in today's world. The capacity to deal with the possible means that the future is now as much of a reality as the present, and it is a reality which can and must be dealt with.[23]

2. Symbols
   a. The adolescent can use symbols for symbols. This capacity makes his thought more flexible than that of the child. Words carry more meaning because they can now take on double meanings; they can mean both things and other symbols.
   b. The cognitive changes in the symbolic process enables adolescents to exert their influence in the domains of humor, irony, and jokes. Adolescents can understand metaphors, double meaning and political cartoons.
   c. During the latter part of the formal period, students begin to grasp double meanings in literature and are also able to understand past whole relationships better.
3. Logico-Mathematical and Scientific Reasoning
   a. Adolescents now have the capacity to combine all variables and find a solution to a problem. They have the ability to determine the effect of one variable on another and the ability to combine and separate variables in a hypothetical, deductive fashion.[7]
   b. They have also developed the ability to use symbols for symbols, to reason inductively and deductively, and to provide generalizations from sorted facts. These elements of formal thought are essential for the study of advanced science and mathematics.

Egocentrism

1. Having discovered capabilities for abstract thought, the adolescent proceeds to exercise them without restraint. In the process of exploring his new intellectual abilities, the adolescent sometimes loses touch with reality and feels that he can accomplish everything by thought alone. The possible and the ideal captivate both mind and feeling and motivate him at times to take on the role of the reformer. He may annoy his elders with all sorts of idealistic schemes. The ideals, however, are almost entirely intellectual, and the young person has little conception of how they might be made into realities and even less interest in working toward their fulfillment. The very fact that ideals can be conceived, he believes, means that they can be effortlessly realized without any sacrifice on his part.[4]
2. Adolescents increased freedom in forming hypotheses often cause them difficulty in making decisions. They see not one but many alternatives open to them. It often leads to external conflict, especially with parents and other authority figures. Adolescents challenge adult de-

cisions, demanding to know the reasoning behind the decision. They are ready to debate the virtue of the parental alternative over that chosen by themselves and their peers.[1]

3. Adolescents caught up in idealism often place their values before those of the family. They take offense at hypocrisy and may rebel against the social structure in a theoretical sense. As the adolescent approaches young adulthood, he usually accepts the reality of social conditions and seeks to solve the pre-existing problems rather than create idealized structures.

Moral Development

1. Higher level moral concepts are based on the adolescent's new cognitive abilities to consider many possible aspects of a problem. Adolescents come to an uncomfortable realization of the complexity of the world.

2. Punishment of a group in order to punish unknown offenders is now viewed as an injustice.

3. Now the adolescent internalizes social values rather than simply imitating them.

4. Adolescents can analyze their own thought processes to gain insight into themselves and also gain insight into the behaviors and intentions of others. They use an imaginary audience as an internal sounding board to mentally try on various attitudes and behaviors.

Not all Adolescents and Adults Function at Formal Thought Levels

1. Research studies suggest that a significant part of our adult population does not attain formal thought. They are handicapped in their ability to think and solve problems.

2. Adolescents and adults:

    a. do not automatically employ formal patterns of thought. Those who do attain this level do not always maintain it consistently. Many people who find themselves facing unfamiliar problems in unfamiliar situations are apt to fall back on a much more concrete type of reasoning.

    b. are more inclined to use formal operations in situations where they have interest, concern, and expertise.

    c. vary considerably in their attempts at thinking. Many want to remain in the comparative comfort of the concrete stage and avoid cognitive challenge.

    d. are trapped intellectually within the cultural system, cultural accomplishments, and expectations.

3. It seems justified to characterize adolescent thought as a separate and organized cognitive level. In any domain, the adolescent is better able to deal with abstract concepts and verbal propositions, appreciate hypothetical possibilities, attend to language for its own sake, and note its ambiguities. Not every adolescent is a formal operator, but every normal adolescent displays some signs of formal operations in science, moral judgement, and literary understanding.[8]

Summary—The Adolescent

1. The adolescent's cognitive development has moved from knowledge through *physical action,* to *symbolic pre-logical intuitive thought,* to *concrete operational* perceptual bound thought, to *formal logical patterns* of reasoning about abstract ideas and problems.
2. The adolescent's cognitive structures have matured to a point where they can effectively *adapt to a wide variety of problems.*
3. The adolescent has the capacity to *think* and to *reason beyond* his own *realistic world* and his own beliefs.
4. He can deal efficiently with the *complex problems* of reasoning, use *probability, possibility, hypothetical,* and *theoretical reasoning* processes.
5. He can *transcend* the *immediate here* and *now,* use propositions rather than sole reality, and reason without reference to concrete experiences.
6. The adolescent is *egocentric* in terms of *not* being able to deal with *idealistic schemes in a realistic way.*
7. He can think of *distant places* and larger and *larger units of space* and can imagine and function in *longer periods of time.*
8. The adolescent can use *symbols* for *symbols;* words take on double meanings.
9. He has the capacity to *combine variables* and do complex scientific and mathematical problems.
10. The adolescent's *moral development* is *tempered* by his new cognitive abilities to consider *many possible aspects* of a problem.

Implication and Application

1. Research indicates that educatorss are not doing a very good job of helping students develop higher mental processes.[2]

2. Teachers:

   a. need to understand the differences between formal and concrete thought processes and promote formal thought as a means of helping students become fully functioning human beings.

   b. need to be able to assess cognitive level and individualize the curriculum to meet the needs of all students.

   c. need to use teaching strategies that allow the student to discover, explore, apply, and internalize concepts and avoid strategies that leave students on lower cognitive levels which require only note-taking, memorization, and regurgitation.

   d. need to use strategies that require thoughtful solutions to problems and synthesis of concepts.

   e. need to remember the value of questions and situations and problems that create moderate disequilibrium.

Bibliography

1. Ambron, Sueann. *Child Development*. New York: Holt, Rinehart and Winston, 1978, p. 161.
2. Boden, Margaret. *Jean Piaget*. New York: The Viking Press, 1980, p. 66.
3. Bybee, Roger W., and Robert B. Sund. *Piaget for Educators*. Columbus, Ohio: Charles Merril Publishing Co., 1982, p. 19, 57, 107.
4. Craig, Grace J. *Human Development*. New Jersey: Prentice Hall, Inc., 1980, p. 363.
5. Elkind, David. "Piaget," Article 26. *Annual Editions: Human Development*. Dushkind Publishing Co., 1982, p. 134.
6. Elkind, David. *Children and Adolescents*. New York: Oxford University Press, 1970, p. xi.
7. Gallagher, J. M. *Cognitive Development and Learning in the Adolescent*, in J. F. Adams (Ed.) Understanding Adolescence (2nd ed.) Boston: Allyn & Bacon, 1973, p. 365.
8. Gardner, Howard. *Developmental Psychology*. (2nd ed.) Boston: Little, Brown and Company, 1982, p. 536, 537.
9. Ginsburg, Herbert and Sylvia Opper. *Piaget's Theory of Intellectual Development*. New Jersey: Prentice-Hall, Inc., 1969, p. 16, 24, 25, 46, 69.
10. Hendrick, Joanne. *The Whole Child*. St. Louis, Missouri: C. V. Mosby Company, 1980, p. 260.
11. Inhelder, B. and J. Piaget. *The Growth of Logical Thinking From Childhood to Adolescence*. (A Parsons and Milgram trans.) New York: Basic Books, 1958. p. 67.
12. Kamii, Constance and Rheta Devries. *Piaget for Early Education*. Chicago, Illinois: Urban Education Research Program, 1973, p. 369.
13. Maier, H. W. *Three Theories of Child Development*. New York: Harper and Row, 1978, p. 45, 82, 87, 88.
14. Phillips, John L. *The Origins of Intellect, Piaget's Theory*. San Francisco, California: W. H. Freeman and Company, 1975, p. 9.

15. Piaget, Jean. *Biology and Knowledge*. Chicago, Illinois: The University of Chicago Press, 1971, p. 147, 148, 155, 241.
16. Piaget, Jean. *In a History of Psychology, An Autobiography*, edited by Edwin G. Boring, Heinz Werner, Herbert Longfeld and Robert S. Yerkes. Worcester, Mass.: Clark University Press, 1971, p. 6, 8, 11, 19.
17. Piaget, Jean. *The Child and Reality*. New York: The Viking Press, 1973, p. 89, 114.
18. Piaget, Jean. *The Judgement of Reason in the Child*. New York: Haracout, Brace and Wold, 1929, p. 71.
19. Piaget, Jean. *The Psychology of Intelligence*. London: Routledge and Keyan, 1950, p. 45, 47, 71.
20. Pulanski, M. A. *Understanding Piaget*. New York: Harper and Row, 1971, p. 41, 84, 105.
21. Stone, Joseph and Joseph Church. *Childhood and Adolescence* (4th ed.) New York: Random House, 1979, p. 189.
22. Travers, John. *The Growing* ., 1982, p. 229.
23. Wadsworth, Barry J. *Piage* Publishing Co., 1978, p. 16, 71.
24. Wadsworth, Barry J. *Piage* vid McKay Company, Inc., 1971, p. 12, 14, 15.

DATE DUE

OCT 2 5 2017			